[page of signatures]

Robert Coles

Tom Harkin

Angeline Lee

Susan Linn

Richard W. Riley

Joe Torre

For all of our grandparents and parents who gave us their legacy,

for all of our children that we now give our own.

And for Carlin Hope McKinnon, to whom I will forever owe mine.

To buy books in quantity for corporate use
or incentives, call **(800) 962–0973**
or e-mail **premiums@GlobePequot.com**.

The Lyons Press is an imprint of Globe Pequot Press.

Text designed by Sheryl P. Kober

Library of Congress Cataloging-in-Publication Data is available on file.

ISBN 978-1-59921-486-3

Printed in the United States of America

10 9 8 7 6 5 4 3 2 1

FSC
Mixed Sources
Product group from well-managed
forests, controlled sources and
recycled wood or fiber

Cert no. SCS-COC-00648
www.fsc.org
© 1996 Forest Stewardship Council

We can succeed only by concert. *It is not "can any of us imagine better?" but, "can we all do better?" The dogmas of the quiet past, are inadequate to the stormy present. The occasion is piled high with difficulty, and we must rise—with the occasion. As our case is new, so we must think anew, and act anew.*

—ABRAHAM LINCOLN

The time has come to reaffirm our enduring spirit; *to choose our better history; to carry forward that precious gift, that noble idea, passed on from generation to generation: the God-given promise that all are equal, all are free and all deserve a chance to pursue their full measure of happiness. . . . We are the keepers of this legacy. . . . Let it be said by our children's children that when we were tested we refused to let this journey end, that we did not turn our back nor did we falter; and with eyes fixed on the horizon and God's grace upon us, we carried forth that great gift of freedom and delivered it safely to future generations.*

—BARACK OBAMA

CONTENTS

DEFENDING AMERICA'S PROMISE))

JUAN WILLIAMS

As we look to the future at the start of the twenty-first century, pollsters are finding a chilling response to the question of "How do Americans feel about America?"

In October 2008, just before the presidential election, only 12 percent of Americans told pollsters for the Pew Research Center that the nation was headed in the right direction. And only 7 percent expressed satisfaction with the current state of the U.S.

That means nearly 90 percent of Americans saw their country going in the wrong direction and over 90 percent reported dissatisfaction with what they saw at that moment as we, the American people, finish out the first decade of the twenty-first century.

These are numbers that pollsters usually find in war-torn countries or in the middle of epidemics of disease or economic depression. We have never seen polling numbers like this in modern America.

After the election there was a revival of spirit. With the inauguration of a new president, Barack Obama, the level of optimism more than tripled according to a Pew poll, with 41 percent of Americans saying they believed the country was on the right track. While that was good news, the majority—59 percent—still said the country was on the wrong track. And there was not a similar, positive jump when pollsters

asked Americans if they were satisfied with the status quo or "with the way things are going." On that question the level of satisfaction went from 7 percent to just 20 percent, leaving 80 percent standing together as unsatisfied.

These poll results came during a recession, on going concern about terrorism, and as the nation continued to fight in an unpopular war in Iraq. But the deeply pessimistic attitudes the polls revealed gave voice to something beyond the immediate difficulties facing the country.

One measure of this is a poll by Public Strategies Inc. released in January of 2009 which found more than half of Americans turning their thumbs down on the future by saying it is not likely or not very likely that "the next generation of Americans will enjoy a better life than we do today."

The sad view of prospects for the next generation of Americans reaches beyond the ups and downs of elections to concerns such as whether the nation's children can expect to live as well as their parents.

Will our children be able to afford the rent on a good apartment or buy a house? Will they be able to get good health care? Will public schools be up to the job of keeping America's children at the forefront of global competition? Will the environment deteriorate to the point of causing natural calamities and shortening life spans? Will the nation ever come to grips with how to control gun violence? Will the American family remain a foundation to nurture the young and the old?

In *Actions Speak Loudest* that deeper level of concern, which hides behind the headlines, is opened and examined by people who have put their hands in the muck and mire of life and tried to create something of beauty—a better outcome. The authors cross all the predictable lines. There are Democrats and Republicans. There are athletes and intellectuals. There is a former president and a queen. Here are people who not only know the statistics but know the reality of these issues.

For example, Richard Castaldo, who was shot at Columbine High School in 1999, discusses gun violence in personal as well as strategic terms. And in this book his essay and all the others is followed by a section on how individuals can take action at home, in their communities, and in the nation to make a difference on gun violence.

Dr. Irwin Redlener, a pediatrician, takes us along for a shocking medical examination inside the mouth of a poor child who has never had the basic medical attention necessary to give him the chance to speak properly. Again, his essay is followed by specific steps that individuals can take

to make a difference in protecting the health of all children.

And Geoffrey Canada, Chief executive officer of the Harlem Children's Zone, Inc., writes with painful firsthand knowledge about the 12 percent of black men who are in jail on "any given day" in America and ties it directly to the fact that 90 percent of them do not have a high school diploma. Again, the essay is followed by suggestions for getting involved with creating solutions to the nation's most important problems.

Actions Speak Loudest is a unique user's guide to making a change. The photographs, by themselves, are inspirational. With the essays and the "action guides," the photographs create a starting point for lifting the American spirit and stirring people to take a risk, make a sacrifice.

This book is in keeping with the American heritage of Paul Revere and his "Call to Action" for true citizens to defend the promise of America. The key idea is to shift the pessimism found in the poll numbers that suggest Americans are getting comfortable with the idea that our children will not have a better life than the current generation.

If you have this book in your hand you are a dangerous American. You have a tool for radical action to make our great country even greater for the greatest gift—our children.

ABOUT *ACTIONS SPEAK LOUDEST*))

In 1908, Congressman William Kent made a generous gift to future generations in giving three hundred acres of beautiful redwood forest to the newly created National Park System. President Theodore Roosevelt wanted the forest to be named after its benefactor, but Kent insisted it be named after the man largely responsible for the creation of the system, John Muir. In declining President Roosevelt's recommendation, Kent wrote, "Your kind suggestion of a change of name is not one that I can accept. So many millions of better people have died forgotten, that to stencil one's own name on a benefaction, seems to carry with it an implication of mandate immortality, as being something purchasable.

"I have five good, husky boys that I am trying to bring up to a knowledge of democracy and to a realizing sense of the rights of the 'other fellow,' doctrines which you, sir, have taught with more vigor and effect than any man in my time. If these boys cannot keep the name of Kent alive, I am willing it should be forgotten."

Inherent in Kent's words is an appropriate definition of legacy. It is our actions that speak loudest in determining the impact of our lives. And while what we leave behind takes many forms, none is so precious or important as our children.

As a new father myself, I have felt the profound sense of responsibility that comes with having a child. My daughter did not come into this world easily, and there isn't a day that goes by when I don't consider how fortunate I am to have her. Implicit in my responsibilities is a pact, an unspoken generational promise that I and all parents make, that says we will go to great lengths and actions to ensure that our children will lead better lives than we have.

Our legacy begins with our own children, but should not end there.

There is an aspect of the American dream that is both self-evident and taken for granted. Inherent in our inalienable rights to life, liberty, and the pursuit of happiness is the belief that in doing so we leave our country and the world a better place because of it. Not just for our children, but for all children.

Progress and prosperity have allowed past generations to keep good on their promise, but today we find ourselves at the crossroads wondering if we will be able to keep it for the next.

The wealthiest nation in the world should have the healthiest children in the world, yet we do not. The most advanced nation in the world should produce the most intelligent and prepared children in the world, yet we do not.

The American family as we've known it is in grave danger. There are almost ten million children in the U.S. without health insurance. Childhood obesity has increased more than 200 percent in the last twenty years. American children are falling behind other countries in educational skills. We are eliminating arts, music, physical education, and history from the curriculum in an attempt to catch up, and their imagination and perspective suffer as a result.

Our youth spend over forty hours a week in front of a screen and fewer than seventeen hours a week with their parents. They are dropping out of organized sports and other community groups at an alarming rate. Every nine seconds, a child drops out of school. They are the first generation of children expected to live shorter lives than their parents. And it can be expected that we will fail in the American ideal to see our children lead happier and more prosperous lives than the ones we did.

When we look forward to what we are leaving behind, not for just the next generation but for the ones that will follow, the picture becomes even bleaker. We are currently in the midst of the most severe global economic crisis since the Great Depression. The world is rife with conflict, and the precious resources that could be going toward solving problems instead go toward creating war. Our planet is in peril, as our resources from energy to food are being used at a rate that fails to consider future generations. Climate change and global warming pose unimaginable consequences. And when in the future troubled times befall our children and grandchildren, the decisions we are making today will compromise their ability to deal with them.

The good news is that we have an unprecedented opportunity to change their future. To still keep our promise, we must have our Scrooge moment of redemption and wake up to realize that the world we see in our nightmares does not have to be.

We live in the wealthiest, most advanced nation in the world. We have the resources—both financial and human—the technology, and the determination to do whatever we want. We have put men in space, defeated time and distance in communications, cured diseases, and saved the world from tyranny. We have done great things before, and we can do them again.

Actions Speak Loudest: Keeping Our Promise for a Better World is a book designed as a clarion call to help us keep our generational promise. It uses the cumulative power of ideas, images, and actions to very simply yet powerfully draw attention to some of the major issues facing America's children, and, most importantly, offer accessible ideas on how to address them.

The issues highlighted in this collection are diverse but share several characteristics. They are serious; they impact a significant percentage of children today, and if not dealt with will have profound consequences not only on individual lives, but also for all of America.

Our contributors are equally diverse, from heroes on the playing field to heroes in the community, from household names to everyday moms and kids. While their backgrounds and political loyalties may be different, they share a common and unquestioned commitment to improving the lives of our children. Their individual legacies have been established not through their words but by their actions, and each offers a testament to the possibilities that lie within us to create a better future for our children.

We have brought these issues and contributors together in one collection because too often we fail to recognize how interconnected they are and how much can be gained by looking at our generational obligation as a whole versus the sum of its parts. The renowned pioneer of dance, Martha Graham, once said, "Every action of ours is passed on to others according to its value, of good or evil, it passes from father to son, from one generation to the next, in a perpetual movement." This book serves to remind us of the intrinsic relationship between our individual actions and this larger movement.

In the different debates addressing children's issues, we've spent too much time pointing fingers and not enough time holding hands. The intent of this book will be to help depoliticize these issues by assembling pieces from all sides and camps, and finding a common ground by focusing not on the politics, but on the children who are profoundly affected by our inability to act. This book hopes to reframe the discussion surrounding these issues away from the "debate" and on to the action that is necessary to improve the conditions in which our youth are being raised.

Each chapter has been designed to allow you—the reader—multiple access points into each issue.

The saying "A picture speaks a thousand words" has been at different times attributed to Napoleon Bonaparte and Confucius. Most people have uttered it at one time or another, and it is something many of us have thought of when moved by an image, perhaps a famous one like Dorothea Lange's "Migrant Mother" or a more personal one from our own families. Given the capacity of the still image to make us feel, each chapter will open with a moving photograph that embodies the human element of each issue.

To test this premise of a picture speaking a thousand words, in this book an essay of approximately a thousand words follows each image. There is no question that a few well-chosen words can equally rally people to act: Thomas Paine's *Common Sense*, Abraham Lincoln's *Gettysburg Address*, or Dr. Martin Luther King Jr.'s "*I Have a Dream*" speech are but three. This book's concept is centered on the hope that the combination of words and pictures will inspire us to take action.

Which brings us to the title of this book. It is inspired by the famous Mark Twain saying whose end is not as well known as its beginning, "Actions speak louder than words, but not nearly as often." Our hope is that in our time our actions will indeed speak *loudest* and with such frequency to create a chorus of change that will ring on from generation to generation.

To help you create your own verse, at the end of each chapter you will find a section also titled "Actions Speak Loudest" which shows how readers like you can become involved in your own homes, communities, and even on a national level to make a difference in the issue at hand.

With great humility, I hope that this book might serve simply as a starting point to a larger movement. As such, while we believe that we have covered many of the major issues of our day and highlighted hundreds of worthy actions and organizations, we also recognize that there may be other issues of import and actions deserving of attention that are not included within these pages. So as you read this book and consider your own legacy, we encourage you to visit www.actionsspeakloudest.org. This online community is a place where you can go to share your own ideas and most importantly actions with other readers and gain more information on how you can help create positive change for children in your own community.

implemented, and others should be pursued aggressively.

We must also strive to correct the injustice of economic sanctions that seek to penalize abusive leaders but all too often inflict punishment on those who are already suffering from the abuse.

The unchanging principles of life predate modern times. I worship Jesus Christ, whom we Christians consider to be the Prince of Peace. As a Jew, he taught us to cross religious boundaries, neighbors have massacred neighbors in Europe, Asia, and Africa.

In order for us human beings to commit ourselves personally to the inhumanity of war, we find it necessary first to dehumanize our opponents, which is in itself a violation of the beliefs of all religions. Once we characterize our adversaries as beyond the scope of God's mercy and grace, their lives lose all value. We deny personal responsibility when we plant land mines and, days or years later, a stranger to us—often

> The bond of our common humanity is stronger than the divisiveness of our fears and prejudices.

in service and in love. He repeatedly reached out and embraced Roman conquerors, other Gentiles, and even the more despised Samaritans.

Despite theological differences, all great religions share common commitments that define our ideal secular relationships. I am convinced that Christians, Muslims, Buddhists, Hindus, Jews, and others can embrace each other in a common effort to alleviate human suffering and to espouse peace.

But the present era is a challenging and disturbing time for those whose lives are shaped by religious faith based on kindness toward each other. We have been reminded that cruel and inhuman acts can be derived from distorted theological beliefs, as suicide bombers take the lives of innocent human beings, draped falsely in the cloak of God's will. With horrible brutality, a child—is crippled or killed. From a great distance, we launch bombs or missiles with almost total impunity, and never want to know the number or identity of the victims.

Citizens of the ten wealthiest countries are now seventy-five times richer than those who live in the ten poorest ones, and the separation is increasing every year, not only between nations but also within them. The results of this disparity are root causes of most of the world's unsolved problems, including starvation, illiteracy, environmental degradation, violent conflict, and unnecessary illnesses that range from Guinea worm to HIV/AIDS.

Most of the work of the Carter Center is in remote villages in the poorest nations of Africa, and there I have witnessed the capacity of destitute people to persevere under heartbreaking conditions. I have come to admire their judgment and wisdom, their courage and faith, and their awesome accomplishments when given a chance to use their innate abilities.

But tragically, in the industrialized world there is a terrible absence of understanding or concern about those who are enduring lives of despair and hopelessness. We have not yet made the commitment to share with others an appreciable part of our excessive wealth. This is a potentially rewarding burden that we should all be willing to assume.

War may sometimes be a necessary evil. But no matter how necessary, it is always an evil, never a good. We will not learn how to live together in peace by killing each other's children.

The bond of our common humanity is stronger than the divisiveness of our fears and prejudices. God gives us the capacity for choice. We can choose to alleviate suffering. We can choose to work together for peace. We can make these changes—and we must.

Jimmy Carter was awarded the Nobel Peace Prize in 2002. As president of the United States (1977–1981), Mr. Carter pursued the Camp David Accords, the Panama Canal Treaties, and the second round of Strategic Arms Limitation Talks (SALT). Jimmy Carter sought to put a stronger emphasis on human rights, and he negotiated a peace treaty between Israel and Egypt in 1979.

After leaving office, Mr. Carter and his wife, Rosalynn, founded the Carter Center, a nongovernmental, not-for-profit organization that works to advance human rights and alleviate human suffering. He has traveled extensively to conduct peace negotiations, observe elections, and advance disease prevention and eradication in developing nations.

((ACTIONS SPEAK LOUDEST: PEACE

Pulitzer Prize–winning author and poet Carl Sandburg wrote, "The single clenched fist lifted and ready, or the open asking hand held out and waiting. Choose: For we meet by one or the other." Peace is the choice we all must make through our actions and the values we pass on. Below are some ways in which you can help kids understand the value of peace and make the choices necessary to wage it.

IN MY HOME
I CAN . . .

Redefine strength.
Teach children that aggression and violence are not examples of strength but rather reflect a shortcoming in a person's ability to handle conflict, and that resorting to violence is often a weakness. Convey to children that real strength is the ability to communicate through a situation. Visit www.teachkidshow.com/teach-your-child-how-to-resolve-conflicts for more information on teaching children communication strategies.

Teach tolerance through empathy and a valuing of difference.
When we choose tolerance we choose the "open asking hand held out and waiting." Visit http://tolerance.org for more information on how you can talk to children about embracing and valuing difference.

Make the costs of conflict real.
During the three-day Battle of Gettysburg, between 46,000 and 51,000 Civil War soldiers died. There are over 250,000 soldiers buried at Arlington National Cemetery, casualties from every war the U.S. has been involved in. Visit these landmark sites and talk to children about the value of peace and the price of its alternative. Go to www.arlingtoncemetery.org, www.gettysburg.com, or www.nps.gov/nhl for a listing of national historic sites.

IN OUR COMMUNITIES
WE SHOULD . . .

Celebrate the International Day of Peace on September 21.
Organize a community event that serves as a first step toward continued commitment to peace. Visit www.internationaldayofpeace.org for more information and suggestions.

Make a short film.
You can organize local kids or students to make a short documentary about the value of peace and incorporate original prose, poetry, and visuals. For more information visit www.peace filmfest.org.

IN OUR COUNTRY
YOU COULD . . .

Check out Peaceful Schools International (PSI).
PSI is a nonprofit organization aimed at promoting a culture of peace in schools throughout the world. They currently have 250 member schools worldwide. Visit www.peaceful schoolsinternational.org for more information on how you can get involved with this global endeavor.

Support the Carter Center.
You can help "wage peace" by supporting the Carter Center, an organization that addresses issues of peace and health that affect the global community. Visit www.cartercenter.org for more information.

Ask your representatives the hard questions.
Legislators have a responsibility to answer the concerns of the electorate. Hold them accountable for the conflicts we enter as a nation. Ask them if they've exhausted diplomatic avenues to resolving conflict.

Perhaps the most obvious was just the way these kids were treated and the way they treated others. Someone told me recently that 30 percent of kids are involved in bullying at school. And frankly that number doesn't surprise me that much. I'm certainly not excusing what they did, but we need to do a better job of getting kids to put themselves in other people's shoes, to think what it might feel like to get picked on or teased all the time and to realize that there are repercussions to these actions.

realized was that in the minds of the killers I was merely collateral damage. Well, I'm not collateral damage any more than innocent Iraqi women and children are.

I guess the reason violence and war offend me so much is because I actually know what it's like to be shot, unlike many of the people who perpetuate violence in the name of our country.

Some say that kids' exposure to violence desensitizes us. Usually when they say this they're again referring to the imagined violence

Maybe it's a better idea to focus our attention not on violent diversions but on the reality of the violent society that we live in.

We don't connect bullying to the violence it can lead to. We think it's just kids being kids. In the same way, we don't connect the violence caused by the adults of our world to the violence caused by kids in our schools or on our streets.

It's really not that surprising to me that something like Columbine happened in this country. In their minds they were wronged by being bullied, so they took it out on the wrong people. It doesn't sound much different than some of our foreign policy decisions since 9/11.

One of the shooters had said that in a war people die. I wonder where he got that idea? He sounds like a hawkish politician explaining away "collateral damage," a euphemistic way of saying we killed some innocent people. The thing I

of games, movies, and music. And that's where they get it wrong. It is the real violence of the world that is numbing. Just turn on the news. What's the old adage that journalists say as if it is a joke: "If it bleeds, it leads."

When I turned on the TV and learned about the Virginia Tech shooting, I have to say I wasn't shocked or surprised. And sadly, I'm sure many other Americans weren't either. What does it say about us when violence or war is an almost expected part of our life? And what message does that send to kids?

I'm no expert on stopping violence, but I do know something about what can happen when you live in a society that doesn't take violence seriously enough. At the expense of sounding clichéd, we just need to be more aware of the environment that we're living in. If we want to stop violence in the hallways of our schools, then we should think about how we use violence in the corridors of power. Yes, we need to teach kids to be more aware of other people, to realize that sometimes hurtful words lead to violent actions. And we need to teach kids that there is no harm in raising their hand to report something that doesn't seem right. But at the same time, shouldn't we also ask the same things of our leaders? After all, this isn't an after-school special; this is real life.

Richard Castaldo is an accomplished musician, songwriter, and composer. His interests are in audio engineering, particularly video game technology. He holds many film and media credits in the industry.

Castaldo is a surviving victim of the Columbine High School massacre, which occurred on April 20, 1999, in Columbine, Colorado. Castaldo was enjoying lunch on the school lawn on the day of the incident. He was paralyzed as a result of the shooting and has since been featured in various interviews, as well as Michael Moore's documentary *Bowling for Columbine*.

((ACTIONS SPEAK LOUDEST: VIOLENCE

On Tuesday, April 20, 1999, Eric Harris and Dylan Klebold walked into Columbine High School and left an indelible mark on the American consciousness. While tragic events like this are rare, bullying, violence among children, and violence in society are not. How do we take steps to ensure that our children are raised in environments absent of the specter of violence? Perhaps the following can help.

IN MY HOME
I CAN . . .

Be aware.
There are several warning signs that can indicate that a child is prone to violent behavior, experiencing violence at school, or just not coping with the violence they may be seeing around them in culture or society. It is important to note that these signs are not definite indicators, but rather things to pay attention to as they can suggest other issues a child may be facing. A good resource to refer to when trying to better understand violence and youth is the National Youth Violence Prevention Resource Center at www.safeyouth.org.

Talk about the difficult topics.
Problems are often foreseeable if adults know what a child is going through, whether it be bullying or trouble adjusting socially. For example, if a child is dealing with a bullying situation, either as a victim or as a bully, show the child healthy ways of dealing with conflict. Go to www.stopbullyingnow.hrsa.gov.

Teach children how to walk in someone else's shoes.
It is critical that children understand empathy and realize they should treat other children how they themselves would want to be treated. A lack of empathy can lead to cruel and abusive behavior, which then can lead to even more violent consequences.

IN OUR COMMUNITIES
WE SHOULD . . .

Create violence-free schools.
School shootings are tragic, but they are also rare. The most common forms of school violence range from aggravated and sexual assault to robbery. These more regular occurrences don't receive national media coverage and are subsequently relegated to the back burner. If you observe an incident, or have knowledge of one, report it to a school official as soon as possible.

Emphasize how important it is that children go to the authorities.
Eighty percent of victimizations go unreported. Our failure in our communities to address comparatively minor (and significantly more frequent) offenses can contribute to escalating violence.

IN OUR COUNTRY
YOU COULD . . .

Convince children to join national antiviolence initiatives like the Student Pledge Against Gun Violence.
Student Pledge Against Gun Violence is a national program that places choice and responsibility in the hands of students and empowers kids in a way that lets them know violence prevention can start with them. Check out www.pledge.org for more information.

Recognize the link between violence in society and violence in our children's lives.
Adults should be prepared to talk about violence in society, its context, and its implications. Major national events such as wars or conflicts in our communities unfortunately set the tone that some youth follow in forming their own perceptions about violence. The nightly news provides critical teachable moments for our youth, and we must challenge our leaders and our media to consider this when violence or conflict is perpetuated or covered.

which the Soviets withdrew their missiles from Cuba while the U.S. quietly did the same from Turkey. Months after, Kennedy created the path to the Partial Nuclear Test Ban Treaty with the Soviet Union, marking the first step back from the brink of global destruction, and therefore a decisive step forward for human survival.

The challenge of our new generation is different from Kennedy's, though the threat of war and the dangerous belief that war is inevitable are the same. We no longer face the threat of imminent annihilation as we did during the height of the Cold War, but we do face the myriad threats of a very crowded planet, pushing up against ecological and cultural constraints. There are irrigation, drought-resistant seeds, anti-malaria medicines, veterinary care for livestock breeders, and other life-sustaining investments vitally needed by all concerned.

We now spend around $1.3 million per minute, $1.9 billion per day, $700 billion per year to finance the Pentagon. A small fraction of that annual sum could ensure universal health coverage of our own people in the United States, and, worldwide, could ensure success in the battle against AIDS, tuberculosis, malaria, and deaths of mothers during childbirth. A small part of that vast annual sum, if invested wisely in the coming years, could deliver to the world the technologies for low-cost solar power, long-mileage automo-

> Peace is the true vocation of successful collective action, the kind of action that builds on the deep commonality of human interests.

6.7 billion people on the planet, roughly twice the population alive during Kennedy's time. Oil, food, and water are increasingly scarce. Human activity is changing the climate in profoundly threatening ways. Like us, the countries of the Horn of Africa, the Middle East, and Central Asia—Sudan, Somalia, Yemen, Iran, Iraq, Pakistan, Afghanistan, and others—need energy, water, food, and a means to address the looming climate changes that are already underway and which will escalate in the future.

There are, however, pathways to peace—to turn swords and spears into the plowshares and pruning hooks of desalination, solar power, drip biles, safe drinking water, and high-yield food supplies, needed to ease the growing tensions on our crowded planet, tensions which threaten the Earth's basic ecosystems, and which also can explode into yet more conflicts over increasingly scarce natural resources in the years ahead.

Indeed, by working with poor and distressed countries in Africa, the Middle East, and Central Asia, not only can we reframe our conflicts into an enterprise of common interest, but we can also help to defuse the underlying hunger, unemployment, and hopelessness that are the tinder of so much violence and extremism today, and which pose direct threats to us as well. And only by working cooperatively with the world on the common challenges of the air, water, species survival, and climate—by making peace with the planet—can we ensure our own survival and the physical basis for the well-being of future generations. In the end, this prophetic vision is about our shared humanity, and the realization that weapons and war rob us of our resources, our hopes, and of course, our very lives. John Kennedy put it this way, in words that I regard as among the most important and beautiful of any uttered by an American leader:

So, let us not be blind to our differences— but let us also direct attention to our common interests and to the means by which those differences can be resolved. And if we cannot end now our differences, at least we can help make the world safe for diversity. For in the final analysis, our most basic common link is that we all inhabit this small planet. We all breathe the same air. We all cherish our children's future. And we are all mortal.

Jeffrey D. Sachs is the director of the Earth Institute, Quetelet Professor of Sustainable Development, and professor of health policy and management at Columbia University. He is also special advisor to United Nations Secretary-General Ban Ki-moon. From 2002 to 2006, he was director of the UN Millennium Project. Sachs is also president and co-founder of Millennium Promise Alliance, aimed at ending extreme global poverty.

For more than twenty years Professor Sachs has been promoting policies to help all parts of the world benefit from expanding economic opportunities and well-being. As director of the Earth Institute he leads large-scale efforts to promote the mitigation of human-induced climate change.

In 2004 and 2005 he was named among the one hundred most influential leaders in the world by *Time* magazine. He is author of hundreds of scholarly articles and many books, including the *New York Times* bestsellers *Common Wealth* and *The End of Poverty.*

(((ACTIONS SPEAK LOUDEST:

COMMON HUMANITY

Our DNA tells us that all humans are 99.9 percent biologically alike, yet too often we fail to see our common humanity. Below are some ways we can take action to make stronger connections between ourselves and our fellow citizens in order to make the world a better and safer one for this and future generations of children.

IN MY HOME
I CAN . . .

Educate my family members about ways to foster understanding.

Teaching peace, compassion, and respect at home ensures that we are able to effectively work with others, understand and respect differences, and create change in the world. The United World College–USA (www.uwcaw.uwc.org) is part of an international educational movement that brings together students from all over the world—selected on personal merit, irrespective of race, religion, politics, and the ability to pay—with the explicit aim of fostering peace and international understanding.

Encourage my children to learn about other cultures.

Bridges to Understanding (www.bridgesweb.org) engages K–12 students worldwide in direct interactive learning to build cross-cultural understanding using technologies such as digital storytelling, live video conferencing, in-person student exchanges, and teacher-led text-based communication.

IN OUR COMMUNITIES
WE SHOULD . . .

Gather community support for organizations that seek to ease the underlying issues that may lead to conflict.

Hunger, unemployment, and hopelessness are often the root cause of violence and extremism today. Millennium Promise (www.milleniumpromise.org) works to implement high-impact programs aimed at transforming lives and ending extreme poverty, hunger, and disease.

Get involved with organizations that engage youth in peace-building activities.

Raising awareness among youth about the consequences of war and conflict can lead to a more positive future for all. Free the Children (www.freethechildren.com) leads projects and campaigns to teach young people to promote peace and end conflict.

Explore nonviolent action in response to conflict as a community group.

The Albert Einstein Institution sponsors programs, research, and resources on strategic nonviolent action for groups fighting for democracy and freedom. Their Web site www .aeinstein.org has information on the uses of nonviolent action and how groups can participate.

IN OUR COUNTRY
YOU COULD . . .

Support the ONE Campaign.

ONE believes in allocating more of the U.S. budget to provide basic needs such as health, education, clean water, and food to help transform the futures and hopes of an entire generation in the world's poorest countries. They value the power of one to make a difference: one person, one voice, or one percent of the U.S. budget. For more information, visit www.one.org.

general insecurity. To counter this, we need to explore ways to use the power of the media to humanize those who are different.

I work with several international initiatives dedicated to addressing this challenge. The Media and Humanity Program of the King Hussein Foundation, which I chair, supports film and media projects that highlight shared values across social, economic, political, and

our understanding of media's impact on interpersonal and intergroup relations.

AOCMF's research was launched in 2008, and complete findings will be released in late 2009, but studies already reveal the influence media has in generating or perpetuating intergroup bias. Media's power over us lies in our capacity to empathize with fictional or nonfictional people we see on the television, movie,

Clearly, words and images powerfully influence our understanding of others—as polarized groups or a common humanity—and this power should not be underestimated.

cultural divides. I also serve on the advisory board of the Alliance of Civilizations Media Fund (AOCMF), an unprecedented initiative created by the United Nations, private media, and global philanthropists to promote and support media content that enhances mutual understanding and respect between different societies and cultures. The AOCMF's work is grounded in extensive scientific research on the neurological, physiological, and psychological responses of viewers to fictional and nonfictional media depicting conflict and humiliation, as well as respect and communication, between polarized groups. These findings will allow AOCMF to build on the accomplishments of pioneers in this field who are already using media for conflict resolution in several parts of the world. They will deepen

or computer screen. If we only see negative or stereotyped depictions of a group, implicit or explicit biases may be activated.

The greater danger may lie in the emotional effects of watching humiliating images of people we identify with. Research has shown that perceived humiliation is experienced neurologically in the same way as real physical pain, and may have the capacity to trigger an intense sense of outrage and an impulse for vengeance with the sole aim of restoring self-esteem. Cross-cultural experiments demonstrate that when individuals are confronted with images of violence against their group, their social identity is strengthened and they are more likely to favor punitive retaliation against the group portrayed as threatening.

While the AOCMF research currently focuses on adults, the implications for children are clear—media that feeds into a polarizing view of the world through stereotypes and misperceptions can prevent our children from understanding and appreciating their place in a vibrant and multicultural world. Humanizing images, on the other hand, can promote healthy self-esteem and encourage improved relations between otherwise polarized groups. In fact, new research shows that this is just where media's transformative power may lie: By viewing images of constructive or positive contact between groups, or counter-stereotypical depictions of diverse lives, we begin to believe in our shared social norms and values. More importantly, we begin to see each other as multidimensional human beings.

Clearly, words and images powerfully influence our understanding of others—as polarized groups or a common humanity—and this power should not be underestimated. Young people everywhere deserve to have access to balanced depictions of those who are different. Together, we must urge media organizations to recognize the impact of the biases they project and to act responsibly. By using the power of media to promote dialogue and understanding, and to build bridges between our societies, we will ultimately enable our global community to see each other as sister and brother.

Her Majesty Queen Noor is an international public servant and an outspoken voice on issues of cross-cultural understanding, peace, and justice.

Queen Noor plays an active role in promoting international exchange and understanding of Arab and Muslim culture and politics, Arab-Western relations, disarmament, and conflict prevention. Her conflict recovery and peace-building work over the past decade has focused on the Middle East, the Balkans, Central and Southeast Asia, Latin America, and Africa.

The initiatives of the Noor Al Hussein Foundation, which she chairs, have transformed development thinking in Jordan and the Middle East through pioneering programs in the areas of poverty eradication, education, women's empowerment, microfinance, health, and arts for social development, many of which are internationally acclaimed models. Queen Noor also chairs the King Hussein Foundation, founded to build on King Hussein's humanitarian vision and legacy in Jordan and abroad through programs that promote education, leadership, and cross-cultural dialogue and media that enhance mutual understanding and respect among different cultures and across conflict lines.

She has published two books, *Hussein of Jordan* and *Leap of Faith: Memoirs of an Unexpected Life,* a *New York Times* bestseller published in fifteen languages.

(« ACTIONS SPEAK LOUDEST: CROSS-CULTURAL UNDERSTANDING

The Gallup Center for Muslim Studies reported that 39 percent of Americans admit to feeling at least some prejudice toward Muslims, and 58 percent of Americans believe Muslims do not care about improving relations. Similarly, a majority of Muslims in Middle Eastern countries have an unfavorable view of Americans. Let's work to reduce these statistics and improve Arab-Western relations today, in hope of making this world a more peaceful place for children tomorrow.

IN MY HOME
I CAN . . .

Identify the similarities between American and Muslim cultures.

In 2006, the Gallup Poll reported that American and Muslim cultures share common values such as a fair political system, respect for human values, liberty, and equality. It highlighted that both cultures criticize "moral and ethical corruption" in the West, as well as excessive personal freedom. Between 74 and 98 percent of Muslim cultures and 68 percent of Americans value religion as an important part of their lives. Read more about the parallel beliefs in Arab and Western cultures at www.gallup.com/consulting/worldpoll/26410/gallup-center-muslim-studies.aspx.

Introduce my children to positive examples of Arab-Western relationships.

Sharing inspirational stories between two cultures is a simple way to create a connection. One example is Greg Mortenson's *Three Cups of Tea,* a beautiful narrative of intercultural trust to help promote peace and education in Afghanistan and Pakistan. Original, young adult, and children's versions can be purchased online at www.threecupsoftea.com.

Reject modern stereotypes and make use of unbiased media outlets to connect my culture with another.

Current stereotypes defined by fear-based images of Arab culture are no fairer than another country's biased portrayal of Americans. Films such as *A Slim Peace, Persepolis,* and *The Kite Runner* provide an honest insight into Arab culture, outside the realms of war. Cinéma Vérité (www.cinema-verite.org) promotes socially conscious cinema and is a great resource for modern global issues. The Alliance of Civilizations Media Fund (www.aocmediafund.org), promotes balanced and accurate depictions of ethnic minorities, primarily focused on Western and Muslim relationships.

IN OUR COMMUNITIES
WE SHOULD . . .

Organize a multicultural fest integrating Arab and Western communities.
Events such as group discussions, food and art festivals, movie nights, or book signings can help to bridge the gap between cultures. Whether it is sharing a handshake, a smile, a common opinion, or a similar interest, multicultural festivals create positive and enriching connections.

IN OUR COUNTRY
YOU COULD . . .

Support organizations promoting peace and conflict resolution between Middle Eastern and Western cultures.
Queen Noor's King Hussein Foundation (www.kinghusseinfoundation.org) advocates for peace and sustainable development in the Middle East. McGill University's Middle East Program in Civil Society and Peace Building (www.mcgill.ca/mmep) has eight rights-based community practice centers in the Middle East focused on advancing social justice and peace building. The Arab West Foundation (www.arabwestfoundation.com) promotes inter-cultural dialogue and understanding.

economic division is sometimes all too evident. On September 11, I looked up from my microscope, where we were trying to isolate the letter "e," to see a plane fly into the World Trade Center, just blocks away. As that day unfurled, my classmates and I watched people jump to their deaths from the burning towers and ran north covered in soot to find safety and reason. The possibility existed to use these tragic events to bring us together and to better understand people of different cultures. Instead we were given more black and white: "good" and "evil," "with us" or "against us."

"second mother" and working with people with backgrounds very different from my own. This gave me insight into the local community—their beliefs and the misunderstandings that can surface based on confusion. At the same time, I always maintained my distinctively American outlook. I was simultaneously an "American" and a "foreigner." In my bridging of a cultural gap, I was not only able to relish the differences of those around me, but also came to a fuller understanding of myself.

Overall, I have learned that it is important for kids growing up to embrace seemingly oppos-

---

It has become all too common to latch onto simplistic labels to describe a person.

When I reached out to diverse societal groups, I began to see how similar we all really are. This became most clear when I looked to different cultures, different countries, and different people, and found less difference than I had expected. This involved volunteering in South America; spending a summer building a fire station in Urubamba, Peru; and later, spending three months in Cochabamba, Bolivia, administering vaccinations while working in a health clinic, where I saw hope bloom from tragedy time and again and perspective born from other people's pain. In South America, within the period of a few months, I was transformed from a complete foreigner to a local, living with a family and my

ing and perhaps curiously juxtaposed interests within ourselves and in the world around us in order to truly understand who we are. The sad thing is that our society today consists of such strong and opposing groups that it prevents us from being defined as anything more than just a one-dimensional "label." Children and young adults are rarely encouraged to take the time to explore how much more interesting and rich life can be—or an individual can be—when these differences are allowed to coexist. Instead, the ever-growing distance between two sides can make it impossible to find the "gray" needed to create a better whole. We must resist accepting when the media fuels these stereotypes: Television shows typically present one-dimensional characters, and news shows highlight polarized opinions, failing to present two sides to a story. Violence and conflict are often the focus of the news, creating an environment of fear and trepidation.

When we are able to defy these stereotypes then we can come to a fuller understanding of ourselves, and ultimately, the world around us. Because without self-awareness, how can we ever hope to understand one another?

This contributor has chosen to remain anonymous. He is currently a senior at a prominent liberal arts college where he is an active member of the community with a broad and diverse array of interests. The experiences detailed in his essay, while unique, come through in words and ideas we can all relate to: a common sense of justice, fairness, and the desire for a world open to the difference we all bring to bear.

(((ACTIONS SPEAK LOUDEST: TOLERANCE

Every day we are placed into neat categories, and we impose those same labels on those we encounter. If we want to foster a world where diversity is affirmed, we need to cherish the diversity within and eschew the limitations of labels. Here are a few suggestions on how.

IN MY HOME
I CAN . . .

Make intelligent choices regarding labels I use and the labels youth are exposed to.
Children model behavior. Avoid pejorative labels and stereotypes, and educate children on what language is offensive and not acceptable whenever they encounter such usage.

Teach children the history of intolerance.
Take the time to teach children about *Brown v. Board of Education,* Dr. King's March on Washington, or Japanese internment camps during World War II. Youth need to understand the ramifications of intolerance. You can visit www.tolerance.org for more information.

Diversify experiences for children.
Teach children to value diversity by having them engage different cultures in fun and informative ways, such as visiting museums, attending performances, or reading literature. Encourage children to ask questions and discuss differences. You can visit www .smithsonianeducation.org/heritage_month for a list of all the heritage months (Black History, Women's History, Hispanic Heritage) and educational resources about them.

IN OUR COMMUNITIES
WE SHOULD . . .

Support school endeavors to affirm difference.

Find out what initiatives local schools have to encourage diversity and community building. From attending forums on gender and sexuality to supporting clubs with various multicultural themes and aims, there are a variety of ways to get involved.

Volunteer at a local teen suicide hotline.

The Centers for Disease Control and Prevention reports that in 2004 suicide was the third leading cause of death for youngsters aged ten to twenty-four. Labels and intolerance alienate youth and compound issues an adolescent might be facing that could make him or her feel more isolated.

IN OUR COUNTRY
YOU COULD . . .

Commemorate the International Day of Tolerance on November 16.

In 1996, the General Assembly of the United Nations invited member states to observe the International Day of Tolerance as an occasion for tolerance education as well as for wider social and political reflection and debate on local and global problems of intolerance. More information about the day as well as resources on tolerance and human rights are available at www.un.org/depts/dhl/tolerance.

in our vehicles and factories, we're causing a dramatic buildup of greenhouse gases in the atmosphere, which is causing global temperatures to rise faster than at any time in the last several thousand years. And because we all play a part in creating the climate crisis, we also share responsibility for creating the solution—not in a linear improvement way, but in a deep, actionable, impactful way.

For-profit business investing in the civic square is good. Corporate funding for critical programs is important. But to truly influence a better future, we need to push public/private partnerships to a point where the results are more impactful than signing a check, being present, meeting expectations. We've got to move beyond being present to being accountable. We've got to consider long-term solutions instead of short-term fixes, and lead the charge on those issues

Where to begin? As the saying goes, "If nothing happens, nothing happens." The way to get beyond linear solutions and back to the business of building civic society and healing the environment is by constantly, continuously applying pressure—to ourselves, to our peers— to innovate, exceed expectations, and imagine new solutions. We should be proud of corporate America's hard-won place in the civic square, but we should also recognize our obligation to continue to earn it. That means viewing corporate responsibility not as a one-time commitment or a marketing ploy, but as an authentic, constant, and critical element of our work—one that we pursue with as much passion and persistence as we do our bottom line.

And although business brings obvious resources to the table, no one gets to take a pass on helping to solve these problems; consum-

> To truly influence a better future, we need to push public/ private partnerships to a point where the results are more impactful than signing a check . . .

that suffer from a lack of leadership. It's easy to disregard those issues that don't have immediate consequences, like global warming, or those that might exist beyond our own boundaries, like hunger and poverty. But the truth is, we have the knowledge and ability—and therefore the responsibility—to create social solutions to the issues that plague our world beyond the here and now.

ers can influence change by making conscious purchasing decisions and demanding greater accountability from the companies they do business with. We need to better educate consumers about their ability to "vote" with their dollars in the marketplace, to influence positive change, and they, in turn, must begin to view ethical corporate behavior as a requirement of doing business, rather than merely a feel-good gift with purchase.

I am a person who believes, as an article of faith, that our greatest hope as human beings lies in an energized civic square that includes all of us. I believe this as the third-generation CEO of a company organized around the notion that commerce and justice are inextricably linked, and as a father who wants to raise my children with an awareness of the world around them. As I see it, we have a choice—a pretty simple one.

We can act on these issues today and create a better tomorrow, or we can continue to ignore them and let them be a cross to bear for the next generation.

Twenty years ago a small group of pioneers was able to redefine the role of business in building community; twenty years later, we've got greater resources and a larger group of pioneers at our disposal to continue to redefine the way in which business can impact positive, sustainable change and help to build civic solutions.

Jeffrey B. Swartz is the third generation of the Swartz family to lead Timberland. Jeff was promoted to president and CEO in 1998, after working in virtually every functional area of the company since 1986. Today, Jeff leads an organization that believes that doing well and doing good are inextricably linked.

Jeff is one of nineteen founding CEOs selected for President George W. Bush's task force on national service called Business Strengthening America. He is on the board of directors for the Climate Group, Share Our Strength, Honest Tea, City Year, the Harlem Children's Zone, and Limited Brands, Inc. In addition, Jeff is a member of the World Economic Forum and the Two/Ten Foundation, an organization providing charitable funds and services to individuals in the footwear industry. In 2002, he received the Two/Ten Foundation's T. Kenyon Holly Memorial Award for Humanitarian Achievement.

(((ACTIONS SPEAK LOUDEST: CORPORATE RESPONSIBILITY

Corporations influence society tremendously, in particular our children. Globalissues.org states that fifty-one of the one hundred largest economies in the world are corporations, not countries. It is a corporation's responsibility to make thoughtful decisions on how their products and services influence customers, suppliers, employees, communities, and the environment. Here are a few ways to ensure ethical consumerism.

IN MY HOME
I CAN . . .

Make responsible choices about the products and companies I invest in.
Consumer products such as the food we eat, the clothes we wear, and the cars we drive represent our vote of confidence in larger organizations. Take a moment to research whether a company's social interests are reflected in their policies and professional actions. Support responsible companies by purchasing their products and services in place of others. Good resources for corporate responsibility rankings can be found at www.business-ethics.com/BE100_all and www.thecro.com/node/615.

IN OUR COMMUNITIES
WE SHOULD . . .

Work with our own companies to practice corporate responsibility.
Utilize the Green Index (www.thegreenindex.com) to determine how green your company is. Eco-friendly efforts preserve the environment around us, making it a healthier place for children to grow and flourish. Organize a community outreach program where employees volunteer at local schools. The nonprofit Everybody Wins! (www.everybodywins.org) partners with companies to increase youth literacy through weekly one-on-one reading sessions in schools.

Support corporations that support our community.

Focusing on corporations within local communities allows you to evaluate and support their efforts to be corporately responsible. Support companies whose interests prevent our children from inheriting larger problems. Their professional goals should support their social actions. In *The High Purpose Company,* Christine Arena praises companies that strive to improve social and economic conditions within their communities, and in doing so, achieve a return on investment: A higher purpose beyond a financial profit. Find out more about the book at www.high-purpose.com.

IN OUR COUNTRY
YOU COULD . . .

Spread the word about environmentally and socially responsible corporations.

Timberland (www.timberland.com/shop/ad4.jsp) created a nutritional label for its footwear with a slogan asking, "What kind of footprint will you leave?" Its unique label focuses on direct environmental impacts such as percent renewable energy, chemicals used, and recycled content. Timberland's model is a great example of how influential corporations can educate consumers about a cause that is at the core of their business and the communities they serve.

Read between the corporate lines.

True corporate responsibility goes beyond powerful advertising and published annual reports. Companies practicing ethical corporate responsibility do in their own offices what they advocate for publicly—for example, recycling if they sponsor a green campaign, ensuring ergonomic conditions when they finance community health, or conserving energy after promoting sustainable energy research. Timberland's Four Pillars of Corporate Social Responsibility (www.timberland.com/corp/index.jsp?page=csr_strategy) acts as a good model. Ask the right questions and do your research before supporting a company's campaign: What do they practice in their own offices? What is the benefit in their campaign to their cause and simultaneously their business?

CLIMATE CHANGE))

BILL McKIBBEN

Henry David Thoreau lived at the very onset of the Industrial Age, and so knew nothing about the destruction wreaked by carcinogenesis or aerosol cans full of chlorofluorocarbons. And though he could perhaps foresee the ruination that greed might cause, he had no inkling that we could damage the ozone let alone warm the globe. "Thank God men cannot as yet fly, and lay waste the sky as well the earth," he wrote. "We are safe on that side for present."

But the sky's not safe after all. We've almost managed to double the fuel efficiency of our cars in the last thirty-five years, but we've also doubled the number of cars, and the miles they drive, spewing out ever-larger clouds of CO_2. Scientists tell us they can see the extra heat, watch it melt glaciers and raise sea levels. To prevent it from getting worse won't require some technical change; it will require doing with less and living more lightly. Our biggest environmental problems—overpopulation, habitat destruction, and so on—will inevitably multiply if we keep living the way we do, continue business as usual, persist in thinking our same thoughts.

A ruined forest near the Grand Canyon, decimated by the increasing number of brush fires; one of the many unintended consequences of rising temperatures associated with climate change. *Robin Bartholick/Corbis*

Global warming is the biggest problem humans have ever faced, and while there are ways to at least start to deal with it, all of them rest on acknowledging just how large the challenge really is.

What exactly do I mean by large? Last fall the scientists who study sea ice in the Arctic reported that it was melting even faster than they'd predicted. We blew by the old record for

over. In Australia things have gotten so bad that agricultural output is falling fast in the continent's biggest river basin, and the nation's prime minister is urging his people to pray for rain. Aussie native Rupert Murdoch is so rattled he's announced plans to make his NewsCorp empire (think Fox News) carbon neutral. Australian voters ousted their old government last fall, largely because of concerns over climate.

> We need to change our sense of what we want from the world.

ice loss in mid-August, and by the time the long polar night finally descended, the fabled Northwest Passage was open for navigation for the first time in recorded history. That is to say, from outer space the Earth already looks very different: less white, more blue.

What do I mean by large? On the glaciers of Greenland, 10 percent more ice melted last summer than any year for which we have records. This is bad news because, unlike sea ice, Greenland's vast frozen mass sits above rock, and when it melts, the oceans rise—potentially a lot. James Hansen, America's foremost climatologist, testified in court last year that we might see sea level increase as much as six meters—nearly twenty feet—in the course of this century. With that, the view from space looks very different indeed (not to mention the view from the office buildings of any coastal city on earth).

What do I mean by large? Already higher heat is causing drought in arid areas the world

What do I mean by large? If we'd tried we couldn't have figured out a more thorough way to make life miserable for the world's poor, who now must deal with the loss of the one thing they could always take for granted—the planet's basic physical stability. We've never figured out as efficient a method for obliterating other species. We've never figured out another way to so fully degrade the future for everyone who comes after us.

We need to change our habits—really, we need to change our sense of what we want from the world. Do we want enormous homes and enormous cars, all to ourselves? If we do, then we can't deal with global warming. Do we want to keep eating food that travels 1,500 miles to reach our lips? Or can we take the bus or ride a bike to the farmers' market? Does that sound romantic to you? Farmers' markets are the fastest-growing part of the American food economy; their heaviest users may be urban-dwelling immigrants, recently enough arrived from the rest of the world that they can remember what actual food tastes like. Which leads to the next necessity:

We need to change our sense of what we want from the world.

We need to stop insisting that we've figured out the best way on Earth to live. For one thing, if it's wrecking the Earth then it's probably not all that great. But even by measures of life satisfaction and happiness, the Europeans have us beat—and they manage it on half the energy use per capita. We need to be pointing the Indians and the Chinese hard in the direction of London, not Los Angeles; Barcelona, not Boston.

In the 154 years since *Walden*, Thoreau has become ever more celebrated in theory and even more ignored in practice. "Men think that it is essential that the Nation have commerce, and export ice, and talk through a telegraph, and ride thirty miles an hour," he writes. How sleepy that protest sounds to an age that thinks we must travel supersonically, communicate instantaneously, and trade globally. Then again, how

sound it seems to an age when we are distracted, depressed, alienated, and over-rushed. He would have understood the jail sentence imposed hourly by the cascade of e-mails into the inbox or the backlog of messages on the voicemail.

And it is here that Thoreau comes to the rescue. He posed two intensely practical questions that must come to dominate this age if we're to make real change: How much is enough? How do I know what I want? The starting point to answering these questions and our current situation is clear: simplify, simplify, simplify. Because if we don't, the temperature of the planet will be higher by 2100 than it's been for hundreds of millions of years, which means crop-withering heat waves, daunting hurricanes, rising seas, and dying forests. The math is hard to argue with; business as usual and growth as usual spell an end to the world as usual.

This is our final exam, and so far we're failing not just for ourselves but for our children and for all future generations. But we don't have to put our pencils down quite yet. We'll see.

Bill McKibben is the author of twelve books about the environment and related issues. His first volume, *The End of Nature,* was also the first book for a general audience about global warming. Appearing in 1989, it has been translated into twenty-four languages. His most recent work, the national bestseller *Deep Economy,* appeared in the spring of 2007. A scholar in residence at Middlebury College, McKibben led the organization of the largest protest rallies in American history about climate change earlier this year; he is co-founder of the current global organizing campaign 350.org. He is a regular contributor to magazines like the *New Yorker,* the *Atlantic, Harper's,* the *New York Review of Books,* and *National Geographic.*

OUR COUNTRY

EDUCATION

TEACHING

HIGH SCHOOL GRADUATION RATES

SCIENCE & MATH EDUCATION

HIGHER EDUCATION ACCESS

HEALTH DISPARITIES

CHILDHOOD OBESITY

DISABILITIES

ECONOMIC SUSTAINABILITY

her career with a salary of $75,000 or more. To attract more of the best and brightest to teaching, we have to face the reality of the job market and make salaries more competitive.

It's clear that we have to pay teachers more while requiring them to work a full year. Perhaps having schools closed for the entire summer worked fine when we had an agrarian society. But today, in failing schools, we need to extend the school year and the school day. That is the only way poor kids can catch up and eventually have a shot at a job in our increasingly knowledge-based workplace. The simple truth is that no one is going to turn around our failing schools with-

I believe that if a child is not succeeding, it is the adults around that child who have failed.

We need to resume the war on poverty with the vigor we would bring to any enemy that threatens our country. Yes, we must win the war on terrorism, but the future of our homeland will never be secure if we continue to lose the war on poverty. Today the country spends, on average, more than $7,500 per pupil annually to educate our children in public schools, while a top private school can cost several times that amount. We do not need to match private schools dollar for dollar, but public schools must do better, and that means greater accountability,

What has been lost is the fundamental belief that the interests of children are first and foremost.

out making teaching in them a full-time job and compensating staff accordingly.

Treating teachers as the professionals they are also means increased accountability for their work with our kids. Right now, a teacher who inspires students can look forward to the same pay raise as the teacher next door who has mentally checked out and is just counting the days to retirement. In fact, great teachers who want to earn more have to leave classrooms entirely for jobs in administration. Our education system needs a structure that fairly rewards great teachers and trains other teachers to improve their classroom skills. And accountability needs to go all the way up the chain of command too.

significantly increased student achievement, and more money, spent wisely.

Certainly the need for improving education, particularly in low-income communities, couldn't be much plainer. Federal, state, and local governments spend $62 billion a year on adult and juvenile corrections. Over the last twenty years, the money spent on prisons was increased by 570 percent while the money spent on elementary and secondary education was increased only 33 percent. We have 12 percent of African-American men in jail on any given day; more than 90 percent of them did not graduate high school.

We can spend escalating amounts of money on jails, drug treatment, and welfare—or we can pay a fraction of that money up front and do the job of educating low-income Americans right the first time.

A child who is intrinsically confident that they have a bright future—and is surrounded by adults who actively reinforce that belief—is going to make it happen. When that occurs today in poor neighborhoods, it is, unfortunately, the exception. We need to make it the rule.

The casualties and ghosts of the abandoned war on poverty sit in our classrooms, walk our streets, and waste away in our prisons. This is truly the American Nightmare: impoverished, uneducated, and unemployable amid a land of plenty. We can continue to ignore them and pay the price or we can call up the national resolve to fight—and through education, win—the country's abandoned war on poverty.

In his more than twenty years with Harlem Children's Zone, Inc., **Geoffrey Canada** has become nationally recognized for his pioneering work helping children and families in Harlem and as a passionate advocate for education reform.

Since 1990, Mr. Canada has been the president and chief executive officer of the organization that the *New York Times Magazine* called "one of the most ambitious social experiments of our time."

In 1997, the agency launched the Harlem Children's Zone Project, which targets a specific geographic area in Central Harlem with a comprehensive range of services. The Zone today covers almost one hundred blocks and aims to serve over eleven thousand children by 2011.

Mr. Canada has written two books: *Fist Stick Knife Gun: A Personal History of Violence in America* and *Reaching Up for Manhood: Transforming the Lives of Boys in America.*

((ACTIONS SPEAK LOUDEST: EDUCATION

Basic education is a fundamental human right, without which all other liberties lose their authority. Many American children are at risk for an enormity of issues due to the lack of protection of this essential right. Below are some actions you can take to help promote and demand basic education in your schools.

IN MY HOME
I CAN . . .

Make my child's education my highest priority.
From the moment of birth to college graduation, make choices and decisions that elevate your child's learning to correlate with their welfare. Provide your child with a proper foundation, and continue to support the steps along the way to ensure the best education possible.

Get involved in my child's school life.
Make it a point to know their teachers, administrators, and friends. Ask them about their day at dinner each night. Some of the multiple benefits of parental involvement include more confidence in school, higher teacher expectations of children, higher teacher opinions of both parent and student, more self-confidence, and children who are more likely to continue their own education.

Create an atmosphere for learning at home.
Dedicate a desk or table to studying, designate time without distractions, and help with homework when asked. Children go further in school when a caregiver supports them in this endeavor both emotionally and mentally.

IN OUR COMMUNITIES
WE SHOULD . . .

Challenge our schools to incorporate family development services and poverty assistance into their offerings.

Recognizing that a child's home life greatly affects their education, work with the Board of Education and school board to ask that schools provide broader services, including parental counseling, free meals, and extended-day options, to ensure each child's well-being.

Form a local support group focused on improving our local public schools.

Collaborate with local government and parents to find solutions for the specific issues affecting your district. Read and interpret whether or not the No Child Left Behind Act has been effective in your community.

Join the PTA.

Essentially, the PTA is a national organization for child advocacy, and by extension, it is a strong supporter for improving teacher quality and reducing class size. The PTA fosters community and provides parents with innovative ways to engage their children and support their teachers (www.pta.org).

IN OUR COUNTRY
YOU COULD . . .

Appeal to your mayor to fund and build charter schools.

Studies have shown education is the key to long-term health in our communities. Petitioning your local mayor is an effective option, as the mayor is directly accountable to the community served by the school and has a unique incentive to fulfill the authorizer's obligation to hold these schools accountable.

Follow congressional legislation centered on education.

Gauge your representative's level of support for public education and educators by visiting www.nea.org. If he or she is not measuring up to your standards, write a letter voicing your concerns and asking for his or her assistance.

degrees is $62,820—about what a teacher might earn with fifteen years of experience. A common misconception holds that teachers deserve less pay because they work fewer hours and get summers off. In reality, however, teachers work long hours after class and during the summers, planning lessons, grading student work, attending classes, and maintaining their credentials. It is no surprise, then, that in a Public Agenda study, 75 percent of teachers considered themselves "seriously underpaid."

Meanwhile, President Bush's education law known as No Child Left Behind insisted that by 2006 all teachers be "highly qualified." A laudable goal, clearly beyond debate. But while school districts must find increasingly qualified teachers, the legislation does not provide enough

and that they be tested yearly to keep their jobs. And he wants all of this without raising salaries a penny. Who would want to work for such an outfit?

This is the question on the minds of thousands of recent college graduates. Talk to students who intend to teach, and ask them how they feel about their chosen profession with this legislation putting teachers under such remarkable scrutiny. Educators must spend a greater portion of their time preparing for standardized tests, and they face reprisals for themselves and their schools if they or their students don't perform correctly. Add to that the prospect that if they're unmarried, or if their spouse doesn't make a good deal of money, their ability to buy a home or car will be limited, unless they take on

> All research points to the fact that the most important component in students' educational experience is the quality of their classroom teacher.

money to substantially increase teachers' earning potential.

Imagine that scenario in the private sector. A chief executive decides he wants better performance from his company. He issues a mandate that all employees be highly qualified. Then he proposes, as No Child Left Behind does, that the staff members be more tightly controlled, that they conform closely to his top-down directives,

that second job. It's no wonder that only 18 percent of recent college graduates say they would ever consider teaching.

There's almost something darkly comic about it all. We place the highest demands on a profession, and not just through the teacher-quality provisions of the legislation. We have unarticulated expectations that teachers be morally and ethically unimpeachable, possessed of

ACTIONS SPEAK LOUDEST

dynamic, compelling personalities and agile minds, and capable of guiding the learning, for example, of thirty-five hormonally charged thirteen-year-olds right after lunch. All research points to the fact that the most important component in students' educational experience is the quality of their classroom teacher.

After asking that of them, we pay them so little that they have to find work selling electronics and cleaning our houses. Is it any surprise that 45 percent of new teachers leave our schools within the first five years?

The solution begins with fixing the legislation and carries down to each school district. Those behind the law have to recognize that schools will never attract the most talented teachers by making the job seem like a cross between a prison guard and the person who administers the written tests at the department of motor vehicles. And districts need to make a commitment to higher salaries; it is the first step in improving not just their schools, but also the community as a whole.

Districts with higher teacher salaries would get the best teachers, families would get better schools, businesses would settle in the city with the great public schools, property values would go up, and everyone would be happy—especially the students, who would get the best educators, gain respect for the profession, and might even consider becoming teachers themselves. The talent pool would then grow ever stronger, and in twenty years we could have created the best corps of teachers the country has ever known.

Dave Eggers is the founder of 826 Valencia, a nonprofit organization providing free literacy and literacy arts services for young people. He is also the founder of McSweeney's, an independent publishing house, and author of several books including his latest novel *What Is the What*. He co-wrote *Teachers Have It Easy: The Big Sacrifices and Small Salaries of America's Teachers* with Nínive Clements Calegari and Daniel Moulthrop.

Nínive Clements Calegari, cofounder of 826 Valencia and CEO of 826 National, is a veteran public school teacher who has had ten years of classroom experience. Before teaching in her family's hometown in Mexico, Nínive worked at Leadership High School, San Francisco's first charter school, where she also served on the board of directors.

Daniel Moulthrop is the host of *The Sound of Ideas,* which airs on WCPN, 90.3 FM, Cleveland, Ohio's NPR affiliate. Before turning to journalism, he taught high school English and a variety of subjects at the San Francisco County Jail.

(((ACTIONS SPEAK LOUDEST: TEACHING

It is important to recognize just how crucial developing and keeping quality teachers in our schools is for the proper education of our children. Below you will find some needed actions to promote this issue.

IN MY HOME
I CAN . . .

Recognize that teachers don't have it easy.

Become educated regarding the plight of many American teachers. Low pay and long hours coupled with little support make the profession a difficult one to stick with. Dave Eggers, Nínive Calegari, and Daniel Moulthrop's book *Teachers Have It Easy: The Big Sacrifices and Small Salaries of America's Teachers* provides great insight into this problem, and provides resources for how you can help. You can also visit www.theteachersalaryproject.org to become more directly involved with their work.

Forge a relationship with my child's teacher.

Many teachers feel underappreciated and overworked; taking the time to acknowledge their efforts can drastically improve their rapport with your child. Studies have shown that children whose parents and teachers work as a team do better in school. Thinking about your child's teacher as your partner can invigorate the learning environment and really make a difference in their education.

Demand the best teachers for my child.

In the last five years, several bodies of research, most notably *What Matters Most: Teaching and America's Future,* published by the National Commission on Teaching and America's Future (NCTAF), have found that teacher quality is the single most important factor in student success.

IN OUR COMMUNITIES
WE SHOULD . . .

Support programs that recruit college graduates to become public school educators.

Teacher recruitment is a central factor in improving teacher quality. There is a high need for educators, especially in urban and rural schools, for subject areas such as special education, math, and science, and for teachers of color. There are several organizations that work to find solutions to this problem, including NYC Teaching Fellows (www.nycteaching fellows.org) and Teach for America (www.teachforamerica.org).

Fight to retain quality teachers.

According to the Board of Education, nearly half of all new teachers leave the field in less than five years. According to a study done by a national task force on education, teachers who leave the field before retirement cite many reasons, most notably poor salaries, poor administrative support, student discipline problems, and lack of aid for professional advancement. Attend PTA meetings and local Board of Education meetings to address these complaints in order to keep good teachers.

IN OUR COUNTRY
YOU COULD . . .

Encourage policymakers to address the issue of teacher quality now.

From a national level, we must insist our leaders find a solution to this incumbent matter through policy renovation and new bills that institute higher pay and higher standards.

Support the Carnegie Foundation for the Advancement of Teaching.

An independent policy and research center whose mission is "to do and perform all things necessary to encourage, uphold, and dignify the profession of the teacher," this initiative fosters collaboration between researchers, teachers, policymakers, and members of organizations with shared interests in education.

Our colleges and universities can also respond to this national economic crisis by recognizing that they have a role to play beyond growing back their endowments. Colleges and universities need to hold the line in raising tuition and help to defray the costs of faculty and students who commit to public service in order to help high school students stay in school until they graduate.

Raising the high school graduation rate should also become a commitment of the community at large. Schools have greater success when they work with the community, universities, and employers to figure out what skills their graduates need to be successful and to provide a bridge from secondary to post-secondary edu-

nections to college credit and employment opportunities. States should provide for the professional development of secondary school teachers and principals so they can learn new ways to engage and hold many more students to graduation, while teaching them meaningful, robust content.

Ultimately, keeping young people in high school comes down to raising expectations and finding ways to engage each young person who is on the verge of dropping out. Local community organizations, schools, and families should create a personalized plan so that every student starting in seventh grade has a high school graduation and career plan that is reviewed and updated every semester by the student, an educator, a family member, and allies in the community.

The annual number of high school dropouts—1.2 million— is twice the size of the U.S. Army.

cation or career training. With the support of community-based organizations, more than a few localities have successfully expanded their alternative education programs. When done well, this leads to coordinated integration of services and encourages a powerful and sustained change in the community.

States set the framework for our local schools. They should encourage small learning communities for middle and high schools. State funding formulas for local high schools should include resources to offer diverse, challenging academic and career courses, extra support, and direct con-

If a student falls off track or doesn't enroll in courses that lead to a better future, mentors, service learning opportunities, and extra help should be provided. We need to find specific ways to engage young people to use technology and to work on teams, skills they will need for years to come. Employers and colleges working with the schools and community groups should plan hands-on visits for struggling students to two- and four-year colleges and job training programs to show them possible paths for their future.

We can also help raise the high school graduation rate by providing more time for learning after school and during the summer. We have little chance of closing the achievement gap if our students remain locked into a six-hour school day and a 175- to 180-day school year.

Above all, our leaders must lift the public debate about public education and college access and encourage the American people to recognize that education excellence is at the very foundation of our economic revival and, indeed, our nation's long-term national security.

This does not necessarily mean top-down reform from Washington but rather a challenge to state and local leaders to step up to their responsibilities. Indeed, in developing a new national consensus, we should work from the bottom up and build on efforts now underway by various schools, communities, and states that are coming together on their own to develop working partnerships. America's strength is our innovation, diversity, competitiveness, and willingness to offer multiple pathways to success. High expectations for all students with high-quality educational opportunities for all students, no matter where they live, promote these core American values.

Richard W. Riley was the U.S. secretary of education from 1993 to 2001, the governor of South Carolina from 1979 to 1987, and a state legislator from 1963 to 1977. He serves as the vice chair of the board of the Carnegie Corporation of New York and of Furman University, where he also chairs the advisory board of the Richard W. Riley Institute of Government, Politics and Public Leadership. Riley also is a board member of the KnowledgeWorks Foundation, a senior fellow at NAFSA: Association of International Educators and co-chair of the National Commission on Teaching and America's Future.

Terry Peterson helps local, state, and national leaders develop strategies, policies, and partnerships to expand learning opportunities and to increase student and school success. He is a senior fellow at the College of Charleston and director of the Afterschool and Community Learning National Network. Terry chairs the national Afterschool Alliance and serves on leadership committees of the national Alliance for Excellence in Education; the National School Boards Association; the Coalition for Community Schools; Foundations, Inc.; and the National Center for Summer Learning at Johns Hopkins University.

Terry has held senior executive positions in state and federal governments. Nationally, he also helped co-found the Arts Education Partnership, the Pathways to College Network, and the Partnership for Family Involvement in Education.

(((ACTIONS SPEAK LOUDEST: HIGH SCHOOL GRADUATION RATES

Every twenty-six seconds a student drops out of high school, creating a nation of young adults who are ill prepared for what lies ahead. **It is imperative that individuals and communities take action to raise the high school graduation rate.** Below are some of the things you can do to help secure the safety of our country's future.

IN MY HOME
I CAN . . .

Keep my children on the right path.

Sit down with your child and help them develop a plan for the future. Setting high, yet realistic, standards can encourage your child to have ambitions and goals, including graduating from high school, college, and having a career. Keep an open dialogue and work with teachers, guidance counselors, and community organizations to broaden your child's support system and ensure your child stays on track.

Help my child through the stresses of high school.

Teens face a barrage of hormonal releases associated with puberty and "massive changes in brain reorganization in preparation for adulthood," according to child psychiatrist June Reynolds. Additionally, increasing amounts of schoolwork, peer pressure, and having to deal with issues like money, alcohol, drugs, and sex can be extremely overwhelming and stressful. Being involved in your child's life can help you provide the support they need to graduate.

IN OUR COMMUNITIES
WE SHOULD . . .

Identify and leverage successful models in school reform.

With the help of organizations like the Bill & Melinda Gates Foundation, new and innovative models across the country are targeting at-risk children and improving the quality of education and high school achievement. Explore bringing Communities in Schools, the Early High School Initiative, KIPP (Knowledge is Power Program) schools, and other progressive programs to your community, or work with local schools to learn from these successful models to help boost graduation rates.

Inspire local high school students.

Work with your company or businesses in your community to create internships, summer jobs, or learning workshops to help high school students see the importance of an education and to develop long-term career goals.

IN OUR COUNTRY
YOU COULD . . .

Support organizations that help America's youth finish high school.

America's Promise Alliance is "the leader in forging a strong and effective partnership alliance committed to seeing that children experience the fundamental resources they need to succeed." At www.americaspromise.org you can find out how to get involved in the local National Dropout Summit, volunteer in other ways, or become a member of the Alliance.

Lobby your state and federal lawmakers to help increase high school graduation rates.

Ask them to support specific programs like the 21st Century Community Learning Centers, GEAR UP, and TRIO that work to make a powerful difference in high school graduation rates through extra learning time and community partnerships. Additionally, experts like Riley and Peterson are advocating for a $10 billion private and federal investment fund to expand proven intervention strategies starting in middle school and to expand successful alternative pathways to graduation. Contact your congressperson to support these types of funds and help our nation's youth.

SCIENCE &
MATH EDUCATION))

BRIAN GREENE

A couple of years ago I received a letter from an American soldier in Iraq. The letter began by saying that, as we've all become painfully aware, serving on the front lines is physically exhausting and emotionally debilitating. But the reason for his writing was to tell me that in that hostile and lonely environment, a book I'd written had become a kind of lifeline. As the book is about science, the soldier's letter might strike you as, well, odd.

But it's not. Rather, it speaks to the powerful role science can play in giving life context and meaning. At the same time, the soldier's letter emphasized something I've increasingly come to believe: Our educational system fails to teach science in a way that allows students to integrate it into their lives.

When we consider the ubiquity of cell phones, iPods, personal computers, and the Internet, it's easy to see how science (and the technology to which it leads) is woven into the fabric of our day-to-day activities. When we benefit from CT scanners, MRI devices, pacemakers, and arterial stents, we can immediately appreciate how

Young schoolchildren visit the American Museum of Natural History and put their hands on the Ahnighito meteorite, the world's second-largest meteorite. *Jonathan Blair/Corbis*

science affects the quality of our lives. When we assess the state of the world and identify looming challenges like climate change, global pandemics, security threats, and diminishing resources, we don't hesitate in turning to science to gauge the problems and find solutions.

And when we look at the wealth of opportunities hovering on the horizon—stem cells, genomic sequencing, longevity research, nanoscience, quantum computers, space technology—we realize how crucial it is to cultivate a general public that can engage with scientific issues; there's simply no other way that as a society we will be prepared to make informed decisions on a range of issues that will shape the future.

As a practicing scientist, I know this from my own work and study. But I also know that you don't have to be a scientist for science to be transformative. I've seen children's eyes light up as I've told them about black holes and the Big Bang. I've spoken with high school dropouts who've stumbled on popular science books about the human genome project, and then returned to school with newfound purpose. And in that letter from Iraq, the soldier told me how learning about relativity and quantum physics in the dusty and dangerous environs of greater Baghdad kept him going because it revealed a deeper reality of which we're all a part.

It is striking that science is still widely viewed

> ## Science is a way of life. Science is a perspective.

These are the standard—and enormously important—reasons many would give in explaining why science matters.

But here's the thing. The reason science really matters runs deeper still. Science is a way of life. Science is a perspective. Science is the process that takes us from confusion to understanding in a manner that's precise, predictive, and reliable—a transformation, for those lucky enough to experience it, that is empowering and emotional. To be able to think through and grasp explanations—for everything from why the sky is blue to how life formed on earth—not because they are declared dogma but rather because they reveal patterns confirmed by experiment and observation, is one of the most precious of human experiences.

as merely a subject one studies in the classroom or an isolated body of largely esoteric knowledge that sometimes shows up in the "real" world in the form of technological or medical advances. In reality, science is a language of hope and inspiration, providing discoveries that fire the imagination and instill a sense of connection to our lives and our world.

In our brief time here on Earth, we've figured out fundamental laws that govern how stars shine and light travels, laws that dictate how time elapses and space expands, laws that allow us to peer back to the briefest moment after the universe began, laws that have allowed us to pry apart the atom and describe its components with fantastic accuracy. These are achievements which, even when only partly grasped, can inspire a deep, life-changing sense of awe and wonder.

And yet, even though we all begin life as little scientists—from the time we can walk and talk we want to know what things are and how they work—so many of us quickly lose our intrinsic scientific passion. And it's a profound loss.

A great many studies have focused on this problem, identifying important opportunities for improving science education. Recommendations have ranged from increasing the level of training for science teachers to curriculum reforms.

But most of these studies (and their suggestions) avoid an overarching systemic issue: In teaching our students, we continually fail to activate rich opportunities for revealing the breathtaking vistas opened up by science, and instead focus on the need to gain competency with science's underlying technical details.

In fact, many students I've spoken to have little sense of the big questions those technical details collectively try to answer: Where did the universe come from? How did life originate? How does the brain give rise to consciousness? Like a music curriculum that requires its students to practice scales while rarely if ever inspiring them by playing the great masterpieces, this way of teaching science squanders the chance to make students sit up in their chairs and say, "Wow, that's science?"

We rob science education of life when we focus solely on results and seek to train students to solve problems and recite facts without a commensurate emphasis on transporting them out beyond the stars.

Science is the greatest of all adventure stories, one that's been unfolding for thousands of years as we have sought to understand ourselves and our surroundings. Science needs to be taught to the young in a manner that captures this drama. We must embark on a cultural shift that places science in its rightful place alongside music, art, and literature as an indispensable part of what makes life worth living.

It's the birthright of every child and it's a necessity for every adult to look out on the world, as the soldier in Iraq did, and see that the wonder of the cosmos transcends everything that divides us.

Brian Greene joined Columbia University as a professor of physics and mathematics in 1996. Professor Greene, a former Rhodes scholar, is widely recognized for a number of groundbreaking discoveries in his field of superstring theory, including the co-discovery of mirror symmetry.

His first book, *The Elegant Universe,* finalist for the Pulitzer Prize in General Nonfiction, sold more than a million copies worldwide. His second book, the bestseller *The Fabric of the Cosmos,* inspired the *Washington Post* to call him "the single best explainer of abstruse concepts in the world today." His latest book is a short story for children, *Icarus at the Edge of Time,* which dramatizes one of Einstein's profound insights in relativity.

((ACTIONS SPEAK LOUDEST: SCIENCE & MATH EDUCATION

On the 2006 International Student Assessment, American students placed sixteenth out of the thirty wealthiest nations in science, and twenty-third in math. This points to a generation of Americans ill equipped to compete in a global marketplace that is more and more defined by technological innovation, or to produce researchers who will address the problems we will encounter in the next century. Below are some ways you can help support science and math in our children's lives.

IN MY HOME
I CAN . . .

Nurture curiosity through teachable moments.

The natural inquisitiveness of kids is pretty conducive to developing a scientific aptitude. Given the frenetic nature of daily life it can be tempting to oversimplify answers or disregard inquiry. Kids then learn to not ask questions rather than to value being inquisitive. Take the time to answer children, and when you don't know the answer, go the extra step and find it with them, or make it real through experiment/experience. You can visit www .kidsites.com for a list of age-appropriate science resources.

Bring more science into the household.

Every day is an opportunity to engage that curiosity and to deepen scientific understanding. Initiate that exploration by going on a hike or challenging kids to think about the everyday world around them in different ways. Expose kids to science media, such as Brian Greene's new black-holes-for-kids fiction book, *Icarus at the Edge of Time.* Check out www.ipl.org /div/kidspace/browse/mas9300/ or http://pbskids.org for kid-friendly science programming.

Bring math into the daily routine.

If you are going out with a small child, ask them to figure things out (how much change you should receive from a small purchase, what the combined price of several items is, or even what the sales tax on an item is). It gives them a chance to develop basic skills and take a certain amount of ownership in their own educational experience.

IN OUR COMMUNITIES
WE SHOULD . . .

Support UTeach.

UTeach (www.uteach-institute.org) is a nonprofit program that seeks to recruit outstanding teachers in math and science in order to address the deficit of qualified teachers in those disciplines.

Advocate for better funding of academic extracurriculars.

Tightened school budgets mean less funding for academic extras like math team, debate, or robotics that supplement classroom learning and nurture academic interests.

IN OUR COUNTRY
YOU COULD . . .

Support national science initiatives.

There are various organizations that are designed to increase American youth proficiency and interest in math and science education. You can look into programs such as the National Math and Science Initiative (www.nationalmathandscience.org) or the Mickelson ExxonMobil Teachers Academy (www.sendmyteacher.com).

selective campuses, you are twenty-five times as likely to run into a rich student as a poor one.

So are rich kids twenty-five times as likely to be born smart as poor kids? No serious people believe that.

No doubt low-income students are less prepared academically than higher-income students: They are more likely to come from educationally disadvantaged homes, to attend lousy schools, and to have SAT scores that lag two hundred points behind those of higher-income students.

According to the congressionally created Advisory Committee on Student Financial Assistance, only 34 percent of low-income eighth graders go on to graduate from high school qualified for college.

The research clearly shows that, controlling for ability, low-income students are much less likely to attend college than high-income students. In a study conducted by John B. Lee, 78 percent of students in the lowest economic quartile and highest achievement quartile as measured by standardized tests had enrolled in postsecondary education within two years, compared with 97 percent of high-achieving students of high socioeconomic status—almost a 20-percentage-point difference. Moreover, 77 percent of students from the lowest achievement quartile and highest socioeconomic status attended college in the same time frame.

Put baldly, the dumb rich kids had as much chance of going to college as the smart poor ones. Another study found that 48 percent of college-qualified low-income students did not attend a four-year college within two years of graduation, compared with 17 percent of high-income college-qualified students.

These data raise serious questions about the role of financial need. The inadequacy of financial aid is the result of conscious decisions by policymakers not to keep up with the rising costs of college. The Pell Grant for low- and moderate-income families, for example, used to cover nearly 40 percent of the average total cost of attending a four-year private college, but now covers about 15 percent.

Colleges, too, are to blame, channeling scarce resources, in order to boost their own rankings, toward financial aid for students who have high SAT scores and families that can afford to pay for their education.

Research by the policy consultant Arthur M. Hauptman finds that, at many private institutions, students from high-income families are nearly as likely to receive aid as students from low-income families.

At selective colleges, another barrier also keeps out low-income students: an admissions system that fails to give them a leg up. Virtually all colleges claim to provide an advantage to "strivers"—students who have overcome tremendous odds to perform quite well. A student from a low-income, single-parent family who attended mediocre schools and managed to do well despite those hardships is generally considered more meritorious than a student who had a comparable or even somewhat better academic record but achieved it with private tutors and all sorts of other advantages.

In reality, however, the rhetoric about providing affirmative action for low-income students turns out to be quite hollow. The Century Foundation study found that the most selective 146 institutions showed racial preferences that essentially triple the combined percentage of black and Latino students to 12 percent from the 4 percent that would be admitted under a system considering only grades and test scores. But the share of students enrolled from the bottom economic half is actually slightly lower (almost 10 percent) than would be admitted under a system of admissions strictly by grades and test scores (12 percent).

There is a rich supply of highly capable low-income students who could do the work at selective universities. The researchers say that at the institutions they studied, a system of "class-based affirmative action"—admission based on grades and test scores with a preference for low-income students—could see the number of students from the bottom economic half rise from the current 10 percent to 38 percent without any decline in graduation rates.

Other researchers have found that even the most elite institutions could substantially increase the number of low-income students without sacrificing quality.

None of this is meant to minimize the enormous issue of preparation. On one level, conservatives are right to argue that K–12 reform is the key to improving college access for disadvantaged groups. But we shouldn't hold our breath for elementary and secondary education to provide genuine equal opportunity any time soon. The problem with the "fix K–12" approach is that it starts a cascade of blame shifting. Higher education blames K–12; K–12 blames its failures on low-income families and inadequate preschool education. Pretty soon, we're all left focusing on the pregnant mother's womb.

By all means, let's work toward adequate nutrition and education for pregnant mothers, and good preschool and K–12 systems too. But inequality in higher education is more complicated than the issue of preparation alone, and colleges and policymakers have crucial roles to play in providing a leg up to low-income students in admissions and ensuring sufficient financial aid. To say the problem is not at all about money is just as silly as to say it's only about money.

Richard D. Kahlenberg is a senior fellow at the Century Foundation, where he writes about education, equal opportunity, and civil rights. He is the author of four books: *Tough Liberal: Albert Shanker and the Battles Over Schools, Unions, Race and Democracy; All Together Now: Creating Middle Class Schools through Public School Choice; The Remedy: Class, Race, and Affirmative Action;* and *Broken Contract: A Memoir of Harvard Law School.* Kahlenberg's articles have been published in the *New York Times,* the *Washington Post,* the *Wall Street Journal,* the *New Republic,* and elsewhere. Kahlenberg has appeared on ABC, CBS, CNN, FOX, C-SPAN, MSNBC, and NPR.

HIGHER EDUCATION ACCESS

((ACTIONS SPEAK LOUDEST:

Robert Wood Johnson's *Commission to Build a Healthier America* states that if all Americans were college educated, it would "result in annual gains of just over one trillion dollars worth of increased health as of 2006." Below are some actions you can take to help promote and encourage higher education.

IN MY HOME
I CAN . . .

Be more involved in my child's education.
To encourage a love of learning, read to your children early on and take them to art and science museums. Helping your children with their homework, hiring a tutor, and being involved in their school life will emphasize the importance of education. Remember to reinforce with positive feedback and celebrate often: a finished book, a newly learned fact, a good test result.

Underscore the importance of college throughout my child's life.
For children who are not academically inclined, you can emphasize the many benefits of a college education—from financial to health to learning important life lessons. Be a good role model and use personal experiences to instill the importance of higher education.

Explore ways to make higher education more affordable for children.
Any relative can start a 529 College Savings or Prepaid Tuition Plan, start a Upromise account, or visit www.salliemae.com/plan to develop an investment plan. Additionally, there are many Web sites and organizations that can help you find scholarships and programs that best fit your children's and family's needs.

IN OUR COMMUNITIES
WE SHOULD . . .

Become SAT or ACT tutors or support tutoring programs.
While finances can be huge barriers for families, inadequate education, inadequate school systems, and lack of family support can also hinder children's ability to attend college. You can volunteer at or support a local tutoring program to help give disadvantaged children the extra attention they deserve.

Encourage economic diversity at higher education institutions.
Universities like Harvard and Georgetown are attempting to level the socioeconomic playing field. You can write a letter to your local college or join/lobby the alumni admissions committee at your alma mater to ask them to close the gap between qualified low-income and affluent students.

Help make higher education possible for other children.
Local community colleges, universities, and scholarship programs need your help. You can donate as an individual or raise money to help lower-income students gain access.

IN OUR COUNTRY
YOU COULD . . .

Encourage policymakers and leaders to support educational programs.
The maximum Pell Grant for the 2008–2009 award year was $4,731, but one year at a private university can cost $38,000. Ask your congressperson to make sure that federal financial aid programs keep up with the rising costs of higher education (http://edlabor .house.gov/ or http://help.senate.gov/).

as an eight-year-old first grader, the die was cast. He would be permanently affected by the label, the developmental "diagnosis," and the consequences of long neglect by his family, community, and school. These would not be easily reversible issues.

The sequence is straightforward: born in poverty, congenital anatomical defect, inability to vocalize properly, no regular primary care doctor, no access to needed specialty medical care, mischaracterization as "delayed," no parental advocate, lack of academic attention, and finally, school failure and elimination of any possibility for reaching his inherent potential. And for all

About nine million of them have no health insurance. For them, getting the care they need is exceedingly difficult, and emergency rooms become the only option. But you can't get your essential vaccinations in emergency rooms. You *can* get acute care when your asthma is out of control and your face is blue and you're coughing your brains out. But you can't get a sit-down with a specialist to see why you're getting the asthma attacks in the first place. And you're not being taught what any middle-class parent in America knows (or should know): that every asthmatic can and should be totally controlled and that being hospitalized for asthma is an

> One in four of our kids . . . face uncertainty, risk, and persistent health problems that impair their future—and ours. . . . This is an imminently fixable problem.

we knew when we saw him on that fall day in Brooklyn, he could well have had a normal IQ. What a waste.

I wish I could say that this was an isolated anomaly, that most kids are getting the care they need. I mean, this is America. But America, it seems, has a big problem. It's about the denial of access to basic services that can help assure that the sublime potential of *every* child is nurtured and cherished.

Here's the actual story.

There are some seventy-five million children under the age of nineteen in America.

abject failure of proper control of the disease. No kid with asthma should be up struggling to breathe—too tired the next day to pay attention in school. Yet that is exactly what is routine and sadly ordinary for kids without appropriate health care.

And then there are the four or five million kids who have some health insurance, but it is very limited. They may well be covered for serious illness and surgery—but not for routine care, vaccinations, and prevention. Or, they may have outpatient coverage, but not for major illness or hospitalization. It's nuts.

Finally, there are probably another five million children who *have* health insurance but face other inexcusable barriers to getting the care they need. Some live in isolated, impoverished communities with few doctors or hospitals. Their insurance cards—mostly Medicaid—are not worth the paper they're printed on if there's no doctor to go to. For others, a clinic *could* be accessible *if* they had a working car or affordable public transportation.

So, what's the total? Figure some eighteen million children aren't getting the health care they need. That's about one in four of our kids who face uncertainty, risk, and persistent health problems that impair their future—and ours. Look, this is an imminently fixable problem. And if the nation's future capacity to compete and thrive matters at all, we'll certainly figure this out. At least that's what I'm counting on.

Dr. Irwin Redlener is professor of clinical public health and director of the National Center for Disaster Preparedness at Columbia University. Dr. Redlener is also president and co-founder of the Children's Health Fund and has expertise in health care systems, crisis response, and public policy with respect to access to health care for underserved populations.

A pediatrician, he has worked extensively in the Gulf region following Hurricane Katrina, organized medical response teams in the immediate aftermath of the World Trade Center attacks on 9/11, and has had disaster management leadership experience internationally and nationally. He is the author of *Americans at Risk: Why We Are Not Prepared for Megadisasters and What We Can Do Now.*

((¢ ACTIONS SPEAK LOUDEST: HEALTH DISPARITIES

There should be no barriers to our children making regular visits to the doctor or receiving the care they need, when they need it. "Children need health coverage so that they receive all the care they need, when they need it, to grow and thrive." Below are actions you can take to help reduce health disparities in the U.S. and improve health care for our nation's future.

IN MY HOME
I CAN . . .

Ensure my children have a medical home.

If your children already have health care, make sure it is "accessible, continuous, comprehensive, family-centered, coordinated, compassionate, and culturally effective." If your child is not insured, visit www.insurekidsnow.gov or call (877) KIDS-NOW to find out if you are eligible for low-cost or free health care coverage through government-funded programs like Medicaid or the State Children's Health Insurance Program (SCHIP).

Instill the value of healthy habits in my home.

Encourage your children to maintain a healthy lifestyle into adulthood. Start by being proactive and don't wait until you or your family is sick, even if you have access to good health care. A well-balanced, nutritious diet, a low-stress active lifestyle, and annual checkups help build the foundation for a healthy family.

IN OUR COMMUNITIES
WE SHOULD . . .

Support organizations that work to provide health care to underserved populations.
The Children's Health Fund is one of many organizations committed to providing health care to the nation's most medically underserved children and their families. Find out how you can make a difference, donate, or get involved at: www.childrenshealthfund.org/getinvolved/index.php.

Work with a community or faith-based organization to bring health education and services to our area.
Families USA (www.familiesusa.org) suggests raising awareness about the importance of screening for health problems and encouraging participation in already-existing public health awareness events.

IN OUR COUNTRY
YOU COULD . . .

Get informed and get involved in the SCHIP reauthorization.
Although SCHIP funding was extended through 2013, there will still be several million children uninsured and several more million who fail to get adequate coverage or health care services. For more information, visit www.cms.hhs.gov/home/schip.asp.

Make your voice heard with state and federal lawmakers to help American children get the care they need.
Stay educated about the important legislation that is being passed, affecting children across the U.S. Visit http://advocacy.childrenshealthfund.org/childrenshealthfund/home/ to learn about the issues and latest news concerning children's health, and sign up to receive e-mail alerts about when and how your involvement can make a critical difference.

We see the early effects in our children. The teasing and bullying some children have to endure is so emotionally stressful some researchers report their moods are as depressed as if they had cancer. And we know that because of their obesity they are likely to develop the health consequences even earlier than people who first became obese as adults. As some have said, our children are in danger of becoming the first generation of Americans to live sicker and die younger than their parents.

While the solution to this epidemic must begin with the personal responsibility of parents and children, this is not the panacea it may seem.

Take the case of Kenyon McGriff. At fifteen, Kenyon weighed over 270 pounds and realized

restaurants, Chinese takeout joints, and corner stores selling packaged foods, cheap liquor, and cigarettes. And the options at his school aren't much better.

"Our school cafeteria is nasty," Kenyon says. "We have burnt pizza every day, hoagies, which are lunch meat slapped on a soggy roll, and then a hot food like chicken nuggets or meat subs."

For millions of children like Kenyon, we need to work harder to make the healthy choice the easier choice.

What if the decisions that were made by our city planners and architects and school leaders were those that encouraged people to be healthy? What if there were wide sidewalks and crosswalks for children to walk to elementary schools that were built inside neighborhoods close to

> When we look around at where we live, learn, work, and play, we find it is as if those places were designed . . . to make becoming obese more likely.

that he needed to choose health. He joined a running club and gave up sugary drinks and greasy fried foods. But like many Americans, he soon discovered the path to good health had many design flaws.

"There's a lot we're missing in this neighborhood. I can't find what I need for my diet."

The streets of Kenyon's urban West Philadelphia neighborhood are dotted with fast food

houses rather than next to highways? What if these neighborhoods had lots of small parks for the children to play in? What if the food served in schools was chosen for its high nutrition and low caloric value, and the only other foods that could be sold in schools had to meet the highest nutritional standards, and the ads children saw on TV or the computer were for healthy foods rather than the least healthy items?

How would we design our neighborhoods, our schools, and our everyday experiences to make our children healthier, like people who own casinos design the casinos to make people gamble more?

Of course, this health disaster facing children like Kenyon today is of our making, affecting us and our children's health, making us less competitive economically and worsening rapidly. In the last analysis all we leave behind are our children and the world they have to live in. If they are less healthy than we were at their age, it is because we didn't make those changes in our schools, towns, states, or nation.

 **James S. Marks**, M.D., M.P.H., directs all program and administrative activities of the Robert Wood Johnson Foundation (RWJF) Health Group as their senior vice president. This includes the foundation's work in childhood obesity, public health, and vulnerable populations.

Prior to joining RWJF in December 2004, Marks retired as assistant surgeon general after serving as director of the Centers for Disease Control's (CDC) National Center for Chronic Disease Prevention and Health Promotion for almost a decade. Throughout his tenure at CDC, Marks developed and advanced systematic ways to prevent and detect diseases such as cancer, heart disease, and diabetes, reduce tobacco use, and address the nation's growing epidemic of obesity.

In 2004, he was elected a member of the Institute of Medicine and currently serves on its membership committee.

CHILDHOOD OBESITY

(((ACTIONS SPEAK LOUDEST:

One in five children from the age of six to seventeen is obese, and an even higher percentage is over-weight. The health complications—mental and physical—that arise in conjunction with obesity are manifold, ranging from hypertension to heart disease, to potentially lowered academic achievement as a result of poor self-esteem. Below are some suggestions on how you can help children manage a healthy weight and live happier, healthier lives.

IN MY HOME
I CAN . . .

Watch the calories going in.
While total daily caloric intake varies depending upon age, maintain a range of 300 to 700 calories per meal for your children. And it is important for these calories to be rich in nutrients that children need to grow. A good first step is to make sure that your children are eating six to eight servings of fruits and vegetables daily and drinking plenty of good beverages like water, milk, or 100 percent juices. Simply replacing highly processed and packaged foods with more natural ones will help ensure that your children are eating the right kinds and quantities of food. The Federal Drug Administration (FDA) has tremendous tools and resources, like the Food Pyramid, that outline the basics of a good diet for our children.

Encourage calories going out.
The other half of the equation is making sure that our children are being active enough. Organizations such as the U.S. Department of Health and Human Services and the National Heart, Lung, and Blood Institute suggest that children get at least sixty minutes of activity most days, if not every day. Make being active a part of your family routine and check out www .healthierus.gov/exercise.html for more ideas on how.

IN OUR COMMUNITIES
WE SHOULD . . .

Get schools involved in the fight against obesity.

Fewer than 8 percent of schools offer daily physical education, and even more are dropping recess from their daily activities. This is compounded by the less-than-healthy foods often found in lunch lines and vending machines, transforming what should be a safe haven for healthy behavior into a potential danger zone. Check out efforts like the Alliance for a Healthier Generation Healthy Schools Program (www.healthiergeneration.org/schools.aspx) for ways to create a healthier in-school atmosphere.

Advocate for health-conscious community planning.

The layout of a community has health implications in regard to whether it promotes physical activity or acts as a hindrance. Advocate for healthy-minded planning of public spaces with better walkways and parks. Visit http://officialcitysites.org/ to find the official Web site of your community. For ideas you can share with them on how to design healthier communities, visit www.cdc.gov/healthyplaces and www.ncsl.org/programs/environ/healthy community.

IN OUR COUNTRY
YOU COULD . . .

Support organizations fighting childhood obesity.

Private foundations like the Robert Wood Johnson Foundation are making tremendous investments in programs that seek to address this public health epidemic. Check out their Web site (www.rwjf.org/childhoodobesity) for information on programs that you might wish to support or bring to your community.

Capitol building, where they demanded a president at Gallaudet who could relate to them as only a deaf person could.

I had the privilege of speaking to the student protesters. I told them, "You are my heroes." They are still my heroes, because they kept up their protests until they won. Gallaudet got its first deaf president, I. King Jordan.

As the chief Senate sponsor of the Americans with Disabilities Act (ADA), there is no question in my mind that the successful protests at Gallaudet were one of the key reasons why, two years later, we were able to pass the ADA with overwhelming, bipartisan majorities in both houses

they have a disability, they have to accept something less, something second best.

Because of Frank's deafness, my family learned basic sign language to communicate with him. And I have always loved the sign for the word "America." All ten fingers are intertwined, joining the hands in a circle. This describes an America where we are not separate, where no one is excluded, where all of us are embraced in a circle, the circle of the American family.

For centuries, kids with disabilities—like my brother Frank—were tragically left out of that circle. But since passage of the ADA, we have learned that America is better, fairer, and richer

---

> I have always loved the sign for the word "America." All ten fingers are intertwined, joining the hands in a circle.

---

of Congress. The ADA was one of the great landmark civil rights laws of the twentieth century— a long-overdue emancipation proclamation for people with disabilities. Thanks to that 1990 law, young Americans with disabilities are entering a new world of greatly expanded possibilities and opportunities.

Today, when I talk to audiences of young people with disabilities, I encourage them to take full advantage of the rights and opportunities that those young people at Gallaudet fought to secure. And, most importantly, I remind them to never allow anyone to tell them that, because

when we make full use of everyone's talents and gifts. Young people with disabilities are mainstreamed in public schools. They are going to college and pursuing challenging careers. They have the same opportunities—and can dream the same dreams—as other young people.

Back in 1990, when I was making the final push to get the ADA through Congress, I met a remarkable young Iowan with severe cerebral palsy named Danette Crawford. She was just fourteen, and one of the brightest people I had ever met. I talked to her about what ADA would mean to her in terms of educational and job opportunities, ensuring that she would not be discriminated against in the workplace.

Danette listened to all this, and in her wonderful way, she said, "That's very nice, very important, Senator. But, you know, what I really want to do is to be able to go out and buy a pair of shoes just like anybody else."

Of course, Danette was exactly right. Young people with disabilities want the opportunity to go to the mall, to go to the movies, and to have fun—just like other kids. Today, thanks to the ADA, they have vastly greater opportunities to do just that. They also have vastly greater opportunities to pursue the college and career of their choice.

We have come a long, long way since the Gallaudet protests in 1988 and passage of the ADA in 1990. I am confident that the upcoming generation of Americans with disabilities will lead us into an even brighter future.

In 1974, **Tom Harkin** was elected to Congress from Iowa's Fifth Congressional District. In 1984, after serving ten years in the U.S. House of Representatives, Harkin challenged an incumbent senator and won. Iowans returned him to the Senate in 1990, 1996, 2002, and again in 2008.

Harkin's signature legislative achievement is the Americans with Disabilities Act of 1990. Known as the "Emancipation Proclamation for people with disabilities," this landmark law protects the civil rights of millions of Americans with physical and mental disabilities. The law has literally changed the landscape of America by requiring accessible buildings and transportation, and workplace accommodations for people with disabilities.

As chairman of the Senate panel that funds medical research, health care, and education initiatives, Tom has worked to transform America into a "wellness society" focused on disease prevention, healthier lifestyles, and good nutrition.

(((ACTIONS SPEAK LOUDEST: DISABILITIES

America has made great strides thanks to the Americans with Disabilities Act (ADA), but there is more to be done. In many ways children with disabilities are prevented from fully participating in activities that most Americans take for granted. Below are some things that you can do to pave the way for the future success of children with disabilities.

IN MY HOME
I CAN . . .

Integrate a child with disabilities into family and household activities.

Studies have shown that children with disabilities tend to be more restricted in their participation in daily activities than their peers. Allowing children to participate more can prevent feelings of isolation and also teach children valuable skills they can use in employment or social activities. *Quest* magazine has published an article with a list of activities that may be appropriate for children with different levels of disability (www.mda.org/Publications/Quest/q123chores.html).

Become informed about disability laws and rights for children with disabilities.

The more you know, the better you can advocate for all children and families. The Special Needs Alliance (SNA) (www.specialneedsalliance.com) is a national, not-for-profit organization of attorneys dedicated to the practice of disability and public benefits law.

Empower a child with disabilities through sport.

Two organizations of many that use sports to help build confidence and empower youth with intellectual and physical disabilities are the Special Olympics organization (www.specialolympics.org) and the National Disability Sports Alliance (www.blazesports.org).

IN OUR COMMUNITIES
WE SHOULD . . .

Work with community establishments to ensure they address the needs of children with disabilities.

Share with business owners and community leaders what you know and alert them to resources they can use to make sure they're in compliance with the regulations of the Americans with Disabilities Act (ADA). The U.S. Department of Justice provides free materials with information about the ADA. Call the ADA at (800) 514-0301 (voice) or (800) 514-0383 (TDD), or access the information online at www.ada.gov/publicat.htm.

Provide support for families in the community.

Offer to provide assistance with child care or other activities, start a support or discussion group if you have experience with children with disabilities, or refer families to resources. The Children's Disability List of Support Groups and Listservs (www.childrensdisabilities .info/speclists.html) is a directory of Internet support groups for families of children with disabilities and special needs.

Volunteer our time with organizations that provide services to children with disabilities and their families.

Family Voices (www.familyvoices.org/index.php), a national grassroots network of families and friends, advocates for health care services that are for all children and youth with special health care needs.

IN OUR COUNTRY
YOU COULD . . .

Connect with schools.

The Individuals with Disabilities Education Act (IDEA) (http://idea.ed.gov) requires that schools offer supplemental supports, aids, and services to make certain that students with disabilities are able to participate in regular education settings with students without disabilities.

groups are actually mutually reinforcing in limiting energy, entrepreneurship, and creativity.

The inspectors general are products of a scandal- and misdeed-oriented mindset, which would bankrupt any corporation. The inspectors general communicate what government employees cannot do and what they cannot avoid. The emphasis is overwhelmingly on a petty dotting the i's and crossing the t's mentality, which leads to good bookkeeping and slow, unimaginative, and expensive implementation.

There are no inspectors general seeking to reward imagination, daring risks, aggressive leadership, and overachievement.

change, we will continue to have an unimaginative, red-tape-ridden, process-dominated system which moves slower than the industrial era and has no hope of matching the speed, accuracy, and agility of the information age.

Clearly, it is simply impossible for the American government to meet the challenges of the twenty-first century with the bureaucracy, regulations, and systems of the 1880s. This process of developing an information-age government system is going to be one of the greatest challenges of the next decade.

As Professor Philip Bobbitt of the University of Texas has noted: "Tomorrow's [nation] state

> **The better you use your resources, the more things you can do. The faster you can respond to reality and develop an effective implementation of the right policy, the more you can achieve.**

Similarly, the members of Congress and their staffs are quick to hold hearings and issue press releases about mistakes in public administration, but there are remarkably few efforts to identify what works and what should be streamlined and modernized. Every hearing about a scandal reminds the civil service to keep its head down.

Similarly, the news media will uncover, exaggerate, and put the spotlight on any potential scandal, but it will do remarkably little to highlight, to praise, and to recognize outstanding breakthroughs in getting more done more quickly with fewer resources. Without fundamental

will have as much in common with the twenty-first-century multinational company as with the twentieth-century [nation] state. It will outsource many functions to the private sector, rely less on regulation and more on market incentives and respond to ever-changing consumer demand."

The better you use your resources, the more things you can do. The faster you can respond to reality and develop an effective implementation of the right policy, the more you can achieve.

An information-age government that operated with the speed and efficiency of modern supply chain logistics could do a better job of providing public goods and services for less money. Our military and intelligence communities would too be capable of buying and using new technologies as rapidly as the information age is going to produce them. Police and drug enforcement would be able to move at the speed of their unencumbered private sector opponents in organized crime, slave trading, and drug dealing. America would finally be able to transform the health system into a twenty-first-century Intelligent Health System that uses information technology to save lives and save money.

We must accept the challenge of creating government programs in each state that can constantly adapt toward better outcomes at lower cost. This approach also might entail providing a bonus to the state that has the best program in the country. It would also create an annual rhythm of benchmarking and data gathering, which would revolutionize how we think about government. Benchmarking would also make very visible the cost of recalcitrant government unions and the cost of bureaucratic resistance to modernization.

We must shift from professional public bureaucrats to professional public entrepreneurs. We must shift from administrators to managers. The metrics will be profoundly different. The rules will be profoundly different. The expectations will be profoundly different.

This is one of the most important transformations of our lifetime, and without it, our children will grow up less safe, prosperous, healthy, and free than we are today. This is also a topic which is just beginning to evolve, but must be treated with the same intensity in the public dialogue as we debate the right policies.

Newt Gingrich is well known as the architect of the "Contract with America" and Speaker of the House from 1995 to 1999. Under his leadership, Congress passed welfare reform, passed the first balanced budget in a generation, and passed the first tax cut in sixteen years.

As an author, Gingrich has published eighteen books including ten fiction and nonfiction *New York Times* bestsellers, including his most recent, *Real Change.*

Mr. Gingrich is founder of the Center for Health Transformation, a collaboration of leaders seeking to establish a market-mediated health care system that will improve choice and quality while driving down costs. In 2007, he became chairman of American Solutions for Winning the Future, a unique non-partisan organization designed to rise above traditional gridlocked partisanship, to provide real, significant solutions to the most important issues facing our country.

(((ACTIONS SPEAK LOUDEST: ECONOMIC SUSTAINABILITY

By transforming government, modernizing the technology that runs many of our nation's institutions, and by implementing the right policies and programs, our country can be more nimble, efficient, productive, and competitive, helping to improve the quality of life for all of our citizens. Below are some ways that you can help the country achieve economic sustainability.

IN MY HOME
I CAN . . .

Make decisions that are economically efficient for my family.

The Federal Reserve Board affirms that American families carry an average debt of $80,000, with over 40 percent owing more than $50,000. When we do not live within our means as individuals, it is difficult to do so as a nation. Therefore, it is important to first make sure that your home finances are sustainable.

Help my children gain fiscal literacy.

Start by educating yourself about how our nation's economy works at sites like www.americansolutions.com, www.concordcoalition.org, or www.operationhope.org. Then share that knowledge with your family. From using tax season as a civic lesson to reading the business and economy sections of the paper together, you can help your children be literate on the federal budget.

IN OUR COMMUNITIES
WE SHOULD . . .

Lobby to help keep our local municipality's budgets balanced.
You can be as familiar with your community's budgets as you are with your checkbook. Contact your local government officials or research local watchdog organizations to educate yourself about how local taxes are being spent and get involved in how these decisions are being made.

Help our local governments be more efficient.
Companies like IBM have developed an e-government initiative leveraging technology and infrastructure solutions that reduce costs and increase efficiency (www-03.ibm.com/industries/government). Additionally, government institutions can learn a great deal from private businesses and entrepreneurs. Work with your company or others in your area to help your community or municipality to be more efficient with operations.

IN OUR COUNTRY
YOU COULD . . .

Engage in federal budget activities.
Acquaint yourself with budget policies and priorities, how federal dollars are spent, and how our economic needs and desires are affected. The National Priorities Project provides data on the impact of federal spending policies for states, cities, and counties, and educates and trains citizens, activists, media, and elected officials on the federal budget, the budget's local impact, and community needs. With this information we can communicate with legislators about our needs and ideas for equitable spending. To learn more, go to www.nationalpriorities.org.

Stand up for where your tax dollars are going.
Citizens Against Government Waste is a private, non-partisan, nonprofit organization whose mission is to eliminate waste, mismanagement, and inefficiency in the federal government. Visit www.cagw.org to find out how you can get involved.

OUR COMMUNITIES

SETTING GOALS

CIVIC INVOLVEMENT

CONNECTING WITH NATURE

FOOD & FAMILY

PHYSICAL INACTIVITY

SCHOOL WELLNESS

FINANCIAL LITERACY

CONFLICT RESOLUTION

SETTING GOALS))

(signature)

| MIA HAMM |

All of my life I've been playing up, meaning I've challenged myself by competing with players older, bigger, more skillful, more experienced—in short, better than me. When I was six, my big brother Garrett ran circles around me. At ten, I joined an eleven-year-old-boys' team, and eventually led them in scoring. Seven years later I found myself playing for the number-one college team in America after becoming the youngest player ever to suit up for the U.S. Women's National Team.

Was I that good? No, but early on coaches detected a competitive fire in me and fed it by continually pitting me against superior opponents. Back then, I wasn't sure I fit in; after all, I was shy and a bit intimidated by players I had idolized. But each day I attempted to play up to their level and earn their respect, and I was improving faster than I had ever dreamed possible.

How many times have parents trotted out the tired old line, "Winning isn't everything," and how many times have you seen children roll their eyes and think to themselves, "Yeah, sure." If winning isn't everything, why is it that we fight so hard to achieve it and feel so empty and

Recent estimates suggest that 80 percent of all nine-year-old children participate in after-school sports teams. By the time they are fourteen that number drops to less than 20 percent. *Philip James Corwin/Corbis*

miserable when we don't? Winning, of course, is as much about how you play the game as it is about who is ahead when the final whistle blows. I'm not about to suggest we teach children how to be good losers; rather, I want them to know how to think and act like winners, whether they come out on top or time ran out while they were still behind. Being a winner is a state of mind, both on and off the field.

Being a winner is pursuing your dreams with energy and determination. I admire dreamers, people who set lofty goals and then go about trying to reach them. We should encourage children to set goals high enough so that it takes effort to achieve them; the goals themselves are not as

Being the best is a simple decision. It's not glamorous. It's not about glory or God-given talent. It's about commitment, plain and simple. But wanting to be at the very top of a field and doing it are two different things. Saying it is exhilarating and a little bit scary because we make a choice to stand out from the crowd; doing it is incredibly hard work. You can't ever live with "good enough." Sometimes deciding to be the best feels great, sometimes it's discouraging, and almost always it's exhausting. The bottom line is that if you don't go into it consistently committed every day, you won't get results.

I find it startling that while over 80 percent of children are participating in some kind of sport

---

Being a winner is a state of mind, both on and off the field.

---

important as the simple fact that they have them and are striving to realize them. Setting goals helps a person's growth and success, otherwise how can you really be sure what you are training for, why you're asking so much of yourself?

Most people have a vague idea in their mind about the future, but uncertainty impedes their ability to achieve greatness. We should encourage children to write down their goals or articulate them. This process will give them focus, help them determine whether those aspirations are really right for them or whether they need to set new ones. Setting out without a direction will lead our youth nowhere, and dreams without follow-through are just that—dreams.

when they are nine years old, by the time they turn fourteen that number drops down below 20 percent! So many children are dropping out for all the wrong reasons. They get too easily discouraged and don't have enough support. I wonder how many realize that Michael Jordan missed over 9,000 shots in his NBA career. That's right, you have to shoot to score.

Once they experience success—and our children and youth will if we encourage them to put in the work—they shouldn't be afraid to celebrate it. Unless they feel good about what they do every day, they won't do it with much conviction or passion. So celebrate what they've accomplished, but also raise the bar a little higher each time they succeed. Once they have achieved something, their confidence begins to build. They realize they're capable of doing it again. But each time they must work a bit harder, because the old saying is true—it is more difficult to stay on top than to get there.

Let them celebrate their victories with exuberance. For too long, society has imposed restrictions on girls and women, telling us that when we achieve something we are not supposed to show excitement and emotion. Take victories, whatever they may be, cherish them, use them, but don't settle for them. There are always new, grander challenges to confront, and a true winner will embrace each one. It is in the journey that our youth will learn the most about themselves. That self-knowledge will help them not only along the way but also beyond, because of course, as they reach one goal, they gain confidence to aspire to the next.

In the end, one of the most important parts of being a winner in life is being happy. A happy person makes those around them happy as well, and that is one of the greatest gifts of all. Help our children make decisions in their life that lead to happiness. I firmly believe that if we allow our children to pursue what they love, they will find happiness. We all know that the pursuit will be filled with its share of hardships and struggles, but if I can follow my life's passion despite all the changes in schools, cities, and friends of my childhood, so can any child.

Let me say now that all those lessons I've shared for our youth—work harder than anyone else, take risks to be a winner, celebrate your victories—will pay off whether or not they ever win a medal, Olympic or otherwise. If we encourage them to go for the goal, they'll always be reaching for a higher place. Each victory is great in and of itself, but champions are on a never-ending quest.

Mia Hamm is widely recognized as the world's best all-around women's soccer player. She was the youngest player ever to play for our National Team (age fifteen) and retired in 2004 after seventeen years, two world championships, and two Olympic gold medals. In April of 1999, Nike named the largest building on its corporate campus after Mia.

In 1997, Hamm's brother, Garrett, passed away from complications related to aplastic anemia, a bone marrow disease, and in his honor she established the Mia Hamm Foundation. The foundation is focused on providing support for two important causes: raising funds and awareness for families needing marrow or cord blood transplants and continuing the growth in opportunities for young women in sports.

Hamm is also is the author of *Go for the Goal: A Champion's Guide to Winning in Soccer and Life* and *Winners Never Quit!*, an inspirational children's book.

((ACTIONS SPEAK LOUDEST: SETTING GOALS

There are few lessons more integral to the future success of youth than the ones gained from the pursuit and attainment of predetermined goals. Kids learn the importance of discipline and dedication, gain the lessons learned in failure, and understand the satisfaction of investment and delayed gratification. Here's how you can set youth on their paths to success.

IN MY HOME
I CAN . . .

Guide kids in setting goals.
Clearly setting achievable goals gives kids a chance to focus and put into perspective what it will take to reach important milestones and long-term aspirations. Googol (www.googol power.com/content/guides/goal-setting-for-kids) has a list of resources on goal setting that you can use to work with children of all ages.

Motivate children to pursue hobbies.
Lifelong hobbies become exercises in proficiency and personal investment. Working with children on a hobby is a good way to spend time and share interests with children. Visit your local library for guidebooks and instruction manuals for hobbies that you and a child can try.

Encourage kids to have fun.
Specialists have argued that kids are more likely to stick with competitive activities and enjoy themselves if they don't have parents pressuring them. The Parent Teacher Association of America provides tips on how you can foster healthy attitudes toward competition. You can find these at www.pta.org under health and wellness in the parent resources.

IN OUR COMMUNITIES
WE SHOULD . . .

Coach youth sports teams.

Get involved in the community effort to support the goals of youth by coaching or volunteering your time with a local youth league. It gives you the opportunity to provide kids with self-esteem and the ability to author a positive self-image. Check out the National Alliance for Youth Sports at www.nays.org to find out how you can best get involved in coaching.

Mentor a child.

Studies have found that mentored young people are less likely to engage in harmful behavior such as illegal drug use or joining a gang and are more likely to get better grades in school, become involved in community service, and raise their goals. MENTOR/National Mentoring Partnership (www.mentoring.org) provides support and tools that those interested in mentoring and others seeking mentoring support can use.

IN OUR COUNTRY
YOU COULD . . .

Donate to organizations that support the goals of youth.

Statistics show that gender inequality persists and girls are disproportionately affected by negative social outcomes. The Mia Hamm Foundation (www.miafoundation.org) seeks to continue the growth in opportunities for young women in sports; 4GGL (www.4GGL.org) aims to change the way in which girls are perceived and treated both globally and locally; and Junior Achievement Worldwide (www.ja.org) educates students on workforce readiness, entrepreneurship, and financial literacy.

Support groups that support young athletes, musicians, artists, and scholars.

Organizations such as Music for Youth (www.musicforyouth.org), American Youth Soccer Organization (www.soccer.org), National Youth Science Foundation (www.nysf.com), and 826 National (www.826national.org) promote skill building and allow kids to pursue creative interests that are both educational and fun.

nurtured and used as the foundation for other forms of social capital and civic engagement.

On the negative side, by every other indicator of civic-mindedness, the younger generation is providing little cause for hope. Just like their parents, young adults are tuning out of civic life. Not only do today's young adults participate in civic affairs less than older adults, but the younger set also participates far less than did its same-age counterparts ten or twenty years ago.

Consider some sobering findings. Every year since the mid-1960s, UCLA has surveyed people are a reflection of who we are as a society and a portent of where we are headed.

It is not merely civic indicators that are down. Young people are far less likely to seek and find social capital in informal settings, such as in the family home or the neighborhood, than were young people a generation ago. Sociologists have found recently that the average American teenager spends more time alone than with family and friends.

Perhaps as a result of this social isolation, the rates of unhappiness, malaise, depression,

> Young people want what everyone else wants: affiliation, community, solidarity, respect, success, and opportunity.

a nationally representative sample of college freshmen to gauge their values and priorities. In the mid-1960s, these young adults were significantly more interested in keeping up to date with politics than they were in making money. Today, those priorities are dramatically reversed. Young adults have also become much less likely to trust other people, support charities, vote, attend community meetings, attend houses of worship, and keep up with public affairs. There are many theories for why the younger generation has dropped out of civic life: the rise in entertainment technology, the selfish values allegedly perpetuated by Boomer parents, etc. Whatever the reason for their apathy, we cannot ignore the fact that young and even suicide have increased among young people. Although suicide has steadily declined among people over forty-five, it has increased dramatically among people under thirty-five. That is not to say that all the news is so dire. In part because of increased prosperity and better public education programs, children's lives have improved in many ways. Compared to a decade ago, young people are less likely to live in poverty (although a fifth still do), less likely to become teenage parents, less likely to be involved in crime or to go hungry, and they are more likely to be enrolled in early-education programs and to get immunized. Doing things *for* our children has risen, even as doing things *with* them has declined. It is less clear whether these positive indicators will lead to similar improvements in these children's sense of well-being and incorporation into community and civic life.

It will not be simple to reverse the generational downturn in civic engagement and social capital. Television and computer technology play a vital role in modern life, and they are here to stay. The challenge to those concerned about dwindling social capital is to embrace the technological and social changes that have brought so much good in recent years, while finding new ways to create social-capital-rich environments for young people in spite of, and ideally because of, these changes. Again, the answer likely will come once we face up to the mismatch between what we expect of young people and the institutions that exist to help fulfill their promise. Never has there been a better time to reengage children at all levels of our social institutions.

The Saguaro Seminar is an ongoing initiative of Professor Robert D. Putnam at the John F. Kennedy School of Government at Harvard University. The project focuses on expanding what we know about our levels of trust and community engagement and on developing strategies and efforts to increase this engagement. A signature effort was the multi-year dialogue (1995–2000) on how we can increasingly build bonds of civic trust among Americans and their communities. The Saguaro Seminar issued the report "Better Together" (www.bettertogether.org) in December of 2000, calling for a nationwide campaign to redirect a downward spiral of civic apathy. Warning that the national stockpile of "social capital"—our reserve of personal bonds and fellowship—is seriously depleted, the report outlined the framework for sustained, broad-based social change to restore America's civic virtue.

((ACTIONS SPEAK LOUDEST: CIVIC INVOLVEMENT

It is becoming increasingly clear that social capital has an enormous array of practical benefits to individuals and to communities. Social capital is built through hundreds of little and big actions we take every day. Below are some things that you can do to strengthen our social capital and increase our civic participation to ensure a positive future for our children.

IN MY HOME
I CAN . . .

Buy a copy of the United States Constitution and Declaration of Independence.
Surveys in the past decade have found that over half of the young people surveyed lack basic knowledge of United States history. Presenting stories about U.S. history in a way that makes it relevant will help the next generation become more informed and improve their capacity for civic participation. Copies of these historical documents can be purchased through the U.S. Government Bookstore at http://bookstore.gpo.gov.

Engage with children in family and school activities.
Sociologists have found that the average American teenager spends more time alone than with family and friends. The availability of social capital at home will improve their well-being and future outcomes. Involve children in family decision-making and attend children's athletic contests, plays and recitals, and other activities.

Encourage children to keep up with public affairs.
Read the newspaper with children and discuss articles about local issues. Also, encourage children to stay informed on their own. *Time for Kids* and its Web site www.timeforkids.com/tfk/kids publishes national and world news, as well as homework help, writing help, and facts and figures about various countries around the world.

Support youth participation in school organizations.
Student groups give students a chance to participate in important school decisions and gain experience in leadership and democracy. The National Association of Student Councils (www.nasc.us) provides a variety of information and resources for current and aspiring student leaders.

IN OUR COMMUNITIES
WE SHOULD . . .

Include children in community-building efforts.
Start a community garden, organize a neighborhood litter pick-up, or plant tree seedlings along your street with neighbors and rotate care for them. The American Community Gardening Association (ACGA) (http://acga.localharvest.org) provides tips, tools, and resources for those interested in community gardening.

Assist in neighborhood youth development initiatives.
Activities geared toward positive youth development will allow children to find much-needed affiliation, community, solidarity, respect, success, and opportunity within their community. Many opportunities exist, such as helping coach Little League or other youth sports—even if you don't have a kid playing. You could also start a children's story hour at the local library.

IN OUR COUNTRY
YOU COULD . . .

Take a child with you when you vote.
Studies have shown that kids who accompany an older family member to the polls are more likely to vote as adults. Those same adults also are more apt to be regular voters themselves and discuss politics regularly with others. Take Your Kids 2 Vote (www.takeyourkids2vote.org) urges parents to bring their children, from toddlers to teens, to the polls when they vote.

otter, beetle, and oak tree. Robin Moore, who is president of the International Association for the Child's Rights to Play, cites such causes as poorly designed outdoor spaces; the rapid growth of domestic air-conditioning since the 1950s; apprehensive parents who keep their children close to home; state-mandated school curricula that do not allow time for study outdoors; and the overly structured lifestyle of many families.

A growing body of evidence indicates that direct exposure to nature is essential for physical and emotional health. For example, new studies suggest that exposure to nature may reduce the symptoms of attention deficit hyperactivity disorder (ADHD), and that it can improve

unstructured dreamtime—to experience nature in a meaningful way. Unless parents are vigilant, such time becomes a scarce resource, not because they intend it to shrink, but because time is consumed by multiple invisible forces, because our culture currently places so little value on natural play. Of course, closing the nature divide is not as simple as making a list. Nor does the solution rest entirely with parents. Parents can work small miracles within their families, but they generally cannot close the divide by themselves. Parents need the help of schools, nature organizations, city planners, and each other.

Nature offers something that the street or gated community or computer game cannot.

> More than anything else, nature is reflected in our capacity for wonder, which makes sense as the word "nature" comes from the Latin root *nasci*—to be born.

all children's cognitive abilities and resistance to negative stresses and depression. Children need nature for the healthy development of their senses, and, therefore, for learning and creativity. This need is revealed in two ways: by an examination of what happens to the senses of the young when they lose connection with nature; and by witnessing the sensory magic that occurs when young people—even those beyond childhood— are exposed to even the smaller direct experience of a natural setting. It takes time—loose,

Nature presents the young with something so much greater than they are; it offers an environment where they can easily contemplate infinity and eternity. A child can, on a rare clear night, see the stars and perceive the infinite from a rooftop in Brooklyn. Immersion in the natural environment cuts to the chase, exposing the young directly and immediately to the very elements from which humans evolved: earth, water, air, and other living kin, large and small. Without that experience, as environmental psychologist

Louise Chawla says, "We forget our place; we forget that larger fabric on which our lives depend." More than anything else, nature is reflected in our capacity for wonder, which makes sense as the word "nature" comes from the Latin root *nasci*—to be born.

We have such a brief opportunity to pass on to our children our love for this Earth, and to tell our stories. These are the moments when the world is made whole. In my own children's memories, the adventures we've had together in nature will always exist. All parents have the same power to make sure that their daughter or son is not the "last child in the woods" but also develops a lifelong relationship with nature.

Richard Louv is an author and journalist focused on nature, family, and community. His most recent book, *Last Child in the Woods: Saving Our Children from Nature-Deficit Disorder,* has stimulated an international conversation about the future relationship between children and nature and has helped spawn a movement that is now moving into the international sphere.

He serves as chairman of the Children & Nature Network, an organization helping to build the international movement to connect children with nature. He also serves as honorary co-chair of the National Forum on Children and Nature. In 2008, he was awarded the Audubon Medal by the National Audubon Society. Past recipients have included Rachel Carson, E. O. Wilson, Robert Redford, and Jimmy Carter.

Louv has written for the *New York Times,* the *Washington Post,* and many other newspapers and magazines.

CONNECTING WITH NATURE

(((ACTIONS SPEAK LOUDEST:

Nature is all around us and so are the opportunities to help our children connect to something so much bigger than us. Below are some simple actions that you can take today to help make that important connection.

IN MY HOME
I CAN . . .

Encourage my children to spend one hour a day in nature.
Studies have shown that children who spend more time in nature tend to perform better academically, are more physically active, and even have lower incidences of attention deficit hyperactivity disorder. The National Wildlife Federation program Green Hour (www .greenhour.org) encourages children to spend at least one hour a day in nature—found in a forest, a city park, or in the backyard.

Seek teachable nature moments.
Every car ride, meal, or hour watching TV is an opportunity to help our children connect to nature. By turning off our daily distractions, we can help children tune in to the world around them and debunk the myth that nature is the past and technology is the future.

Take my family on a nature vacation.
Trips to national parks or camping can establish the love of the outdoors and the profound sense of wonder that accompanies it at an early age. Yet trips to parks have dropped by 25 percent since 1987 and most people who visit a park don't venture more than a quarter mile from their cars.

IN OUR COMMUNITIES
WE SHOULD . . .

Integrate nature into our children's school experience.

Recently, the U.S. House of Representatives approved the No Child Left Inside Act of 2008. Contact your local legislature to see what you can do to help implement environmental education in your schools.

Remove the barriers that inhibit our children's connection to nature.

It is important that communities help parents understand the realistic risks associated with being outside. Fear of injury and stranger danger are often not substantiated by the facts, as a recent study by Duke University found this to be the safest time in our history to raise children.

Plan more child-friendly neighborhoods.

It is important that we encourage our community planners to incorporate walkways and bike trails, unlinked to roads, which enable families and children to recreate and travel safely.

IN OUR COUNTRY
YOU COULD . . .

Join the Children & Nature Network.

Go to www.cnaturenet.org for more information on this issue and to see how you can become more involved in the "no child left inside" movement.

Support groups that support nature.

Groups such as National Geographic, the Sierra Club, and the National Wildlife Federation are among many that seek to enhance, protect, and restore nature where it exists and bring it into the places where it is missing. Many of these groups have youth-directed efforts to engage them in nature.

small amount of money and buy a large amount of inexpensive food, a whole chicken, root vegetables, grains, and pastas, and I could provide myself with decent meals for an entire week. When you are able to enjoy a meal every night you won't feel like a "have not." Your life will feel richer, whether or not there is a big roll of cash in your pocket.

Cooking is a lifelong skill that will allow you to share with those around you and explore other cultures, people, and places by trying flavors or new recipes. As I grow older, I find food comforting. It reminds me of my past; the older you get the more comfort you get out of cooking. The legacy becomes richer.

A friend told me once when you choose to give back, make it personal. Food is the way I started in the kitchen while making meals that are easy, healthy, affordable, and delicious. We want to help parents and kids enjoy cooking together and to break down the myth that cooking is hard or confusing. We believe that parents and kids will make better food choices if given the opportunity, knowledge, confidence, and realistic options to do so. Lives are so busy today. Food choices should be easy and realistic. Parents should have the tools to cook good food for and with kids.

Yum-o! also helps kids reach their food-related career goals by funding scholarships and recognizing public schools that are offering food or nutrition programs that incorporate healthy choices. We accomplish this through our partnerships with the National Restaurant Associa-

> In a country with so many financial and food resources, there is no excuse for so many of our children and families to be suffering from hunger.

make my living, so food should be the way I give back. I have seen firsthand how food plays an important role in our lives. I started the Yum-o! organization with these goals in mind: to end hunger for America's children; to provide a scholarship program for children who want to explore a career in the restaurant and food service industries; and to raise families' awareness about food and cooking—enabling them to get tion Educational Foundation and the Alliance for a Healthier Generation. Together with Feeding America and their network of food banks, and Share Our Strength, we are donating funds to food communities coast-to-coast, and creating awareness about the issue of hunger. The Yum-o! Web site (www.yum-o.org) is the central place where Yum-o! provides tools and resources for young cooks, such as recipes and tips for the kitchen.

"Yum-o!" is the sound you make when you eat something really super delicious. It's kind of a combination of "yummy" and "oh wow!" You can't help but smile when you say it because it's such a fun word to say. A big part of the Yum-o! organization is about making cooking and eating something that makes people happy. Food should be delicious, fun, and put a smile on your face.

Every day every child should experience the smile that good food brings. It is nourishment that is necessary not just for their short-term physical growth but for their long-term emotional happiness.

Rachael Ray is an iconic Food Network television personality, bestselling cookbook author, and editor-in-chief of her own lifestyle magazine, *Every Day with Rachael Ray*. In the fall of 2007, she launched the top-rated and Emmy Award–winning daytime program *Rachael Ray*.

Ray has turned her "30-Minute Meals" concept into a bestselling series of cookbooks. Her five most recent titles all hit the *New York Times* bestseller list in the first month on sale. *Newsweek* has praised Ray as being "the most down-to-earth TV star on the planet," and *Business Week* honored her as one of the "Best Leaders of 2006."

In 2006 Ray founded Yum-o!, a nonprofit organization that empowers kids and their families to develop healthy relationships with food and cooking by teaching families to cook, feeding hungry kids, and funding cooking education and scholarships.

((ACTIONS SPEAK LOUDEST: FOOD & FAMILY

Our relationship with food is often one of negotiating unhealthy extremes. Millions of American children over-consume, while many go hungry. Below are a few suggestions on how you can help ensure all American children lead healthier lives through a healthy relationship with food.

IN MY HOME
I CAN . . .

Eat meals with a child.

A study conducted by Project EAT found that when a family eats meals together, adolescents are less likely to be overweight, smoke, or use drugs. For time-saving, fun, healthy recipes visit www.yum-o.org.

Increase my family's nutritional literacy.

Processed foods are typically high in calories, sugar, sodium, and preservatives and often don't offer the nutrients growing bodies need. If you want children to adopt healthy eating habits, give them the information and food options they need to do so. Replace prepackaged snacks with fruits and vegetables. Teach children how to make healthier choices. Spot the Block (www.spottheblock.com) is a resource for kids to learn how to read nutritional information on food labels.

Make food fun.

Healthy eating doesn't have to seem like a chore. Preparing, cooking, and especially eating food with the family should be a blast. Have fun with it, share your favorite food stories from your childhood, and teach children interesting tips and tricks about food that your parents taught you.

IN OUR COMMUNITIES
WE SHOULD . . .

Advocate for a food co-op or organic market.

Make healthier food choices a reality for your neighborhood by advocating for healthier foods on shelves. One way to do that is to be directly involved in those decisions. You can visit http://cgin.coop/how_to_start for more information on food co-ops.

Volunteer at a local soup kitchen.

Sixty percent of homeless women have children under the age of eighteen. Take a child with you to volunteer. It can be the first step toward a continued dedication to civic service. You can visit www.kidzworld.com/article/5060-serving-up-soup-at-a-soup-kitchen for a kid-friendly explanation of soup kitchens. To find one near you contact your local school, community center, or house of worship.

Organize a food drive.

One of the simplest and most effective ways to address the issue of hunger is to organize a food drive, collecting non-perishables that you can donate to any soup kitchen or church.

IN OUR COUNTRY
YOU COULD . . .

Advocate for stricter FDA regulations.

You can lend a voice to how the FDA determines its guidelines. If you feel changes need to be made in how the FDA makes decisions regarding food labels, acceptable preservatives, etc., you can visit www.regulations.gov and voice your opinion.

Support funding and initiatives for healthier food options.

You can help raise awareness about the issue of hunger by getting involved with or donating to Feeding America (http://feedingamerica.org), which has a network of over two hundred food banks serving all fifty states, and Share Our Strength (www.strength.org). Additionally, you can visit www.yum-o.org/how_cool_archive.php to learn more about other organizations dedicated to improving the way we eat.

Think back to your own youth for a minute. Were your parents active? Did they tell you that you needed to be active for sixty minutes each day? Did they encourage you to go outside and play? Now think back to your school: Did you have daily physical education or recess? If you answered yes to any of these questions, chances are you developed pretty good habits about staying active. Unfortunately, for too many kids today, the answer to most or all of those questions is no.

Children should be encouraged to play . . . to take breaks . . . to hydrate . . . to refuel. Often the rest they are told to take by their parents is to help the parents manage the situation. The older

Hydration isn't a reward for practicing well. It is a necessity to keep the body functioning well.

The same goes for food. I won't get into what and why some foods are healthier than others. But the fact is, you need to feed your body well for it to function at its best.

That brings me back to the most important point: physical activity.

Physically, competition often brings out the best in people. I was lucky to grow up enjoying competition. My brother and I would compete for everything. We used to compete all the time: basketball, football, first one to wake up, first one to the dinner table. So for us, getting up and

> It is easy for a child to see how we enjoy ourselves. What they see, then, can become what they decide to do themselves.

we get the more we slow down. Kids don't need to do that. They, like all of us, need to be active.

These days there is a constant stream of new information about health. It's amazing to me how times have changed, and how much more we know about how to stay healthy. Here's an example.

When I played in youth leagues, we were told that we could have a "water break" during practice at a particular time. The whole team stopped practice and had a few minutes to drink water before practice resumed. If we didn't take advantage of that break, we would not have another chance for a drink until after practice. That method was not unique to my team but was standard operating procedure back then. Today, there are rules against such procedures.

running around, lifting weights, whatever, was easy; it was part of our everyday activity.

It is not that easy for everyone. So many adults get caught up in the daily grind and neglect themselves. They don't eat properly; don't exercise at all; ignore what the doctors instructed them to do. It's not just unhealthy, it sets the wrong kind of example for children. I have family members who struggle with their weight, who look at working out as a means to an end and not something they relish. But they do it. They have come to a point where they have to.

For children, there can be even more barriers to being active. Some neighborhoods are not conducive to playing, either because they are unsafe or because there is no access to parks or playgrounds.

When they go to school, they aren't given opportunities to be active either, as fewer and fewer kids in public schools are offered daily physical education classes. Unfortunately, in this country there are many overweight people. Their weight has led to other ailments such as diabetes, high blood pressure, heart failure, and back and joint pain. There is an expression that the older you are, the harder it is to take it off. That is so true. And it's not looking any better for the next generation. It is sad to think that less than half of today's children meet the recommended amount of physical activity.

It all starts at a young age. Learning the proper way to eat and embracing an active lifestyle are habits to be formed early in life. As a parent, I know one of the most important things I can do for my children is to help them develop healthy habits early.

Even as more information becomes available, no one will ever know everything there is to know about health. Things change; the environment changes; our bodies change. But the basics stay the same: the importance of staying physically active and being smart about the food we put into our bodies. Not just for yourself, but because our kids are watching and learning from us. You want them to be healthy, smart, and respectful, among many other positive characteristics. You don't need to be a professional athlete to set a good example. Being active shouldn't be a chore. The enthusiasm I feel as a pro quarterback throwing a touchdown pass is the same kind of feeling I had when I was running around the backyard at the age of ten.

It's our responsibility to value healthy eating habits and staying physically active, and to communicate this to our children. Not just by what we say, but also through what we do and how we do it.

A first-round draft pick in 1999 by the Philadelphia Eagles, and the second player overall, Donovan McNabb has raised the bar with superstar accomplishments on and off the playing field.

At only thirty-three years old, he has established himself as one of the finest players in franchise history. He holds the franchise records for pass attempts, completions, passing yards, and touchdown passes. McNabb has already piloted the club to more wins (eighty-two), postseason games (twelve), and postseason victories (seven) than any other quarterback in team history.

During his career, McNabb has quarterbacked the Eagles to the postseason seven times, won the NFC East Division five times, played in four consecutive NFC Championship Games, and led the team to their first Super Bowl berth in twenty-four years.

But some of his proudest gains can be found off the field. A great personality combined with a sense of humor and extraordinary work ethic has spilled into his community efforts through the Donovan McNabb Foundation (DMF). His primary focus is on diabetes awareness and prevention.

((ACTIONS SPEAK LOUDEST: PHYSICAL INACTIVITY

A recent issue of the *Journal of the American Medical Association* reports that "moderate to vigorous physical activity" drops by as much as one-third in youths between the ages of nine and fifteen. This trend of decreasing activity inversely tracks the upward trend of obesity, heart disease, and earlier occurrences of Type 2 diabetes. The combination of nutrition-poor, high-calorie diets and sedentary lifestyles fuels an epidemic of weight-related health complications. Below are some suggestions as to how you can inspire kids to lead healthier, active lifestyles.

IN MY HOME
I CAN . . .

Play.
The National Heart, Lung, and Blood Institute suggests that kids get at least sixty minutes of moderate to vigorous physical activity most days if not every day. Make it more fun and be a role model by playing with kids. There are various programs such as the NFL's Play 60 (www.nflrush.com) or EmpowerME (www.empowerme2b.org) with great advice for how kids can stay active.

Allow kids to find their own activity niche.
Nurture an interest in physical activity, whether it be Little League or ballet. Suggest fun activities for kids to get involved in, without pressuring them.

Make activity-conscious purchases.
Make purchases that will inspire kids to be more physically active. Better yet, make purchases you both can enjoy together, such as baseball mitts, a Ping-Pong table, or a football. You being a part of it is just more incentive.

IN OUR COMMUNITIES
WE SHOULD . . .

Join the International Walk to School event.
Register your community or local school to take a step toward a more active lifestyle. Visit www.walktoschool-usa.org.

Push for better playgrounds and facilities.
Hearts and Parks, a program started by the National Heart, Lung, and Blood Institute, supports local initiatives to create better recreational environments for kids. Visit www .nhlbi.nih.gov and type "Hearts N' Parks" in the search bar for more information. Also visit Kaboom (www.kaboom.org), an organization dedicated to building playgrounds in under-resourced areas.

Get involved in active volunteering.
Volunteer in ways that get you moving, such as rehabilitating parks and gardens. Or, you can help in a big way with Habitat for Humanity, building homes for those who need them. For more information visit www.habitat.org.

IN OUR COUNTRY
YOU COULD . . .

Become a part of national movements for recess and physical education.
For many students recess is a fading part of their daily routine. Join a national movement to promote recess in public schools. Visit the International Play Association (www.ipausa .org), the National Institute for Play (www.nifplay.org), or check out www.rescuingrecess .com and www.sports4kids.org for more information.

in "education reform" for almost forty-five years, and yet the somewhat dismal state of many of our children and young adults today tells us we are still a long way from reaching these goals.

In retort, and sometimes in defense, many education professionals involved in reform maintain that a healthy community school system can only be attained if those schools operate in healthy communities with "ready to learn" children, thereby enabling teachers to teach to their potential and students to learn to their potential. That no doubt is true also . . . hence, the conundrum. So, the "reality question" from educators is what do we do if the community is

coordinated school health, and parent and community involvement, not revolving curricula and endless testing and pressure.

The second realization is that public school people have to first *not* do something. We must refrain from blaming, although there is plenty of blame to go around; however, the reality again is that kids are coming to school tomorrow just like they came today—no fairy godmother is going to sweep into their lives overnight to make them okay! So, we have to change our service delivery to address the barriers to learning that our children come to school with in today's society. No more excuses for us; we have to use the

> We all say that one has to be healthy to learn, but we forget that our children have to first learn how to be healthy and be given the opportunity to be healthy.

not healthy? How do we get our children and teachers into a position to have a shot at being successful for all children, not just some?

The very first realization for all of us "on the ground" trying to make education work, trying to "leave no child behind," is that education reform is controlled largely by political contributors, lobbyists, book companies, curriculum makers, and high-stakes testing contracts. They control because we don't stand up and wrest that control away, although we know their version of reform has failed us. No matter to them . . . they have gotten very wealthy off of our inaction. The research speaks to early childhood education,

research we know in order to prepare a generation of young people for opportunity.

Meeting the basic needs of our children and staff is the basic answer in this quest. We have to do for all the children what we strive every day to do for our own children. The basic needs are the same for all children, but the meeting of those needs is not.

The social scientist Abraham Maslow said that physical health, safety, being nurtured and loved, and having a sense of positive self-esteem are all needed in order to learn most effectively and to achieve independence. Coordinated school health is the major avenue in schools for meeting those needs. It includes health services, health education, physical education, staff wellness, nutrition, safety, community and parent involvement, and counseling and mental health services. This program provides for our children the basic human needs that they may not be getting anywhere else in their world. And the resiliency research bears out the fact that if we can give a child these things somewhere in his life, then his chances of being successful are immensely enhanced.

We all say that one has to be healthy to learn, but we forget that our children have to first learn how to be healthy and be given the opportunity to be healthy. For "success for all learners" and "leave no child behind," the battle cries of politicians and school reformers alike, to become a reality, schools and their communities have to figure out a solution for providing those basic needs to all of our children. In my mind, coordinated school health is a large part of that solution.

As an educator for over thirty-three years, and administrator for the past twenty-four years, I have come to the conclusion that there is no more effective way to approach true success for all children: black, white, rich, poor, able, and disabled. And the data is there to substantiate that claim. Children come to school many times with problems and burdens they bring from their homes and communities. We have to acknowledge the presence of those barriers to learning, but we cannot use those problems as excuses not to teach them effectively.

I believe that most educators feel that we have tried most everything commercial and professional during the last forty-plus years of education reform. Some have worked for some students, but most have failed for many. It's those many that are hurting us in our society. Our choices as educators are to either keep on plugging under duress and stress or to take control of the situation by addressing those potential barriers to learning. The former choice will make us sick. The latter will give us back that feeling we all had when we started our education careers, a sense of hope and accomplishment. Coordinated School Health will do that.

Dr. Pat Cooper currently serves as the chief executive officer of the Early Childhood and Family Learning Foundation in New Orleans, Louisiana. The goals of the foundation include establishing community centers in the most economically depressed and crime-ridden neighborhoods of New Orleans.

Just prior to the New Orleans appointment, Dr. Cooper served as superintendent of schools in McComb, Mississippi. He served in that capacity for ten years and is in his thirty-eighth year of public education service. While in McComb, the McComb School District implemented a planned thirteen-year longitudinal study relative to the relationship of coordinated school health programs to school reform.

Prior to becoming superintendent in McComb, Cooper served four years as executive director for the CDC-funded National School Health Education Coalition (NaSHEC) in Washington, D.C.

((ACTIONS SPEAK LOUDEST: SCHOOL WELLNESS

The idea of school wellness encompasses the availability of choices and educational strategies regarding those options that contribute to the health of students. These concerns range from nutrition to physical activity to choices adolescents make regarding sex. Below are some suggestions on how you can supplement school wellness and further ensure healthier future generations.

IN MY HOME
I CAN . . .

Know how well schools are.

In 2004 Congress passed the Child Nutrition and WIC Reauthorization Act, which stipulated that all schools receiving federal funding for school meals must implement a set of policies regarding nutrition and physical activity by the 2006–2007 academic year. Go to www.schoolwellnesspolicies.org for more information on those policies.

Ask what kids eat in school.

The demands of a busy life may make it difficult to send kids to school with a homemade lunch. You can be proactive in asking what your kids eat every day to help them make better decisions about what they put into their bodies. Request weekly menus from your child's school and talk with kids about choices.

Supplement physical education in schools.

The Centers for Disease Control and Prevention recommends at least sixty minutes of moderate to vigorous physical activity preferably every day. The Model School Wellness Policies developed by the National Alliance for Nutrition and Activity requires only 225 minutes a week. You can add to this by engaging in physical activity with a child outside of school.

IN OUR COMMUNITIES
WE SHOULD . . .

Make sure schools have healthy alternatives in vending machines.
Organizations such as Alliance for a Healthier Generation are working to ensure that students are provided with healthier food options and can make healthier nutritional choices to improve overall health and wellness. Visit www.healthiergeneration.org to find out how your school can get involved in this movement.

Start a fundraiser to help purchase physical education equipment.
A recent article in *Edutopia* reports that some school districts are having parents pay for resources that diminished budgets can no longer afford. Raising funds to compensate for shrinking budgets can help physical education departments purchase and maintain the equipment and facilities students need to stay healthy. You can read the article at www .edutopia.org/beyond-bake-sales-family-subsidy-public-schools.

Advocate with local school boards for Coordinated School Health Programs (CSHP).
A CSHP model consists of eight interactive components: health education, physical education, health services, nutrition services, counseling and psychological services, healthy school environment, health promotion for staff, and family/community involvement. Together, these components create and maintain the overall health and well-being of children and ensure academic success.

IN OUR COUNTRY
YOU COULD . . .

Support the work being done by the Centers for Disease Control Department of Adolescent and School Health (DASH).
Visit DASH's Web site (www.cdc.gov/HealthyYouth) to find valuable information and resources on the role that schools play in improving the health of our children. And if you like what you see, make sure you contact your local congressmen to tell them how valuable their work is to our children.

the perspectives of high school dropouts, approximately one-third of all children, and 50 percent of minorities, in public high school drop out of high school nationwide. In many of the nation's "dropout factories," the percentage of dropouts far outpaces the percentage of graduates.

This is not good for twenty-first-century America, and it is an economic death sentence if not changed for black, brown, and low-wealth communities nationwide, or almost 100 million Americans. Can we afford to write off almost 100 million Americans, or approximately a third of our nation's population? Who is going to fund our Social Security fund in retirement if we do? Hello?

is the means by which students move from simply avoiding the poverty trap to embracing a true prosperity agenda for themselves, their families, and their communities.

With respect to our kids, we all need to make "smart sexy again," because we have sure succeeded at making dumb sexy over the past twenty years or so. My friend Quincy Jones told me recently that it takes twenty years to create a culture. What kind of culture have we created among our young people over the past twenty years? Are we proud of that? Really?

The book *The Tipping Point* notes that communities that are relatively stable have 5 percent

> Without question, education is the ultimate poverty-eradication tool.

My experience growing up in an inner-city neighborhood shows that these are not dumb kids. These are simply misdirected kids. Kids who have somehow lost their way, are low on hope and self-esteem, and unfortunately, kids who also don't believe that education is relevant to their futures.

I believe that one way to show kids the relevancy of education is to teach them the language of money at an early age. To link education with aspirations, and to show kids how they can get rich, legally. That's the power of financial literacy, or what I see as the first step in our growing "silver rights" movement, and the power of education, too.

Without question, education is the ultimate poverty-eradication tool, for when you know better you tend to do better. But financial literacy

or more of role models within them, from doctors to lawyers to accountants to bankers and such. And so, from say the 50 percent role model level all the way down to a mere 5 percent, a community is stable. That's inspiring to me. As little as 5 percent. But, at 3.7 percent role models in a community, irrespective of race, everything negative explodes, from teen pregnancies to crime to, yes, high school dropout rates.

What's the magic of 3.7 percent you ask? My guess is that at 3.7 percent the most hopeful young person cannot remember, reflect upon, understand, or even appreciate meaningfully what a real role model looks like; and so no wonder every urban, inner-city young person I meet these days wants to be a rap star, an athlete, or, God forbid, a drug dealer. It makes sense, actually. These are not dumb kids. They are modeling precisely what they see.

No, we are not talking about dumb kids. These kids are very smart. Example: I think drug dealing is one of the most morally offensive and disgusting "businesses" ever imagined, and when caught the perpetrators should go straight to jail. Period. Now, this said, you cannot be a dumb successful drug dealer. Yes, I said it.

If you pursue this immoral trade (of drug dealing), and you are somehow good at it, you are not dumb. You are wrong as two left shoes, but you are not dumb. You understand finance, marketing, distribution, customer service, market penetration, territory, pricing, wholesale, retail, profit margins, and maybe import and export too. No, these kids are not dumb nor stupid, but simply misdirected, and in need of hope and a practical sense of opportunity in their lives.

As a result of the bad choices that many of these immensely bright kids have made in their lives, most of them will probably never be able to secure a meaningful job at a major Fortune 500 company (which conducts background checks), but they can become entrepreneurs. Heck, they are already entrepreneurs.

What if we unleashed upon America, and the world, a new vision for the twenty-first century, an ambitious generation of role-model-inspired, positive and contributing young entrepreneurs, self-employment projects, and "doers" over the next twenty years? I'll tell you what would happen: America would get a genuine second shot at keeping this party called American prosperity going over the next one hundred years, because you cannot keep a third of the American population on the economic and aspirational sidelines and otherwise expect that it will.

There is a difference between being broke and being poor. As I often say, "Being broke is a temporary economic condition, but being poor is a disabling frame of mind and a depressed condition of one's spirit," and we must vow to never, ever be poor again.

John Hope Bryant is a social entrepreneur whose work to empower the underserved has earned him the role of vice chair of the U.S. President's Advisory Council on Financial Literacy and chairman of the council's Under-Served Committee. He is the founder, chairman, and chief executive officer of Operation HOPE, America's first nonprofit social investment banking organization and a leading national self-help provider of economic empowerment tools and services for the underserved. Since its founding in 1992, Bryant has raised more than $400 million in lending commitments for low-wealth homeownership and small business creation. He works in active partnership with more than 390 banks, insurance companies, credit unions, and corporations, along with government and community leaders.

((ACTIONS SPEAK LOUDEST: FINANCIAL LITERACY

Debt has become a staple in many American households (more children watch their parents file for bankruptcy than for divorce), while annual surveys, such as the one conducted by the Jump Start Coalition for Financial Literacy, reveal how little high school students know about basic fiscal responsibility and strategies. Given the uncertainty of the financial future, the next generation must be equipped with the financial know-how to ensure its own security.

IN MY HOME
I CAN . . .

Start teaching financial literacy early on.

There are simple ways to set the stage for sound financial strategies early on. Impressing upon kids the importance of budgeting, or setting up a savings plan with something as easily accessible as a piggy bank, can go a long way in forming good financial habits. Visit Operation HOPE's Banking on Our Future financial literacy program (www.operationhope .org/smdev/clst4.php?id=172) for tips on how to teach children basic financial literacy.

Teach children investing.

The lessons learned through investment go beyond financial security. These lessons demand that children learn the difference between short- and long-term goals, as well as the discipline required to track growth. Visit www.360financialliteracy.org for more information on the benefits of investment-teaching and how you can have a child gain some firsthand experience.

Make financial responsibility a reality.

Allow children to learn the importance of financial responsibility by making it real. Make kids follow a strict budget. If they want to make any extra purchases it should come from money they have saved. Financial responsibility over a limited sum of money forces children to reevaluate how much they spend and fosters a more critical approach to future spending.

IN OUR COMMUNITIES
WE SHOULD . . .

Support funding for financial literacy.

Financial literacy should be mandatory for every child in America, but particularly for low-wealth young people who may lack proper role models. Speak to your local legislator about how this can be done.

Start a fundraiser/clothing drive/can drive.

Philanthropy is as much a matter of financial literacy as savings. It places consumption and materialism in perspective. It further emphasizes the notion of community and that our decisions, economically and socially, are mutually linked.

Join the 5 percent movement.

If 25,000 or more Americans committed one hour a month, twelve months a year, volunteering (as a HOPE Corps volunteer, for example: see www.operationhope.org/smdev/lf1.php?id=592), we could stabilize the necessary baseline of 5 percent role models.

IN OUR COUNTRY
YOU COULD . . .

Join the silver rights movement.

John Hope Bryant has articulated that we are moving from a civil rights movement toward a "silver rights" movement, a movement with the premise that investment and creation of a financially literate population will provide communities hardest hit by poverty with the means to secure their economic future. Become a supporter of Operation HOPE at www.operationhope.org.

can happen," says therapist Michael Gurian, an expert on adolescent male development and author of *The Minds of Boys*. "Emotions are meant to be experienced, expressed, and expelled. Violence can become one way of doing all three." Conversely, girls are more likely to verbalize their feelings, even when they get very angry. "Girls talk a lot, that's sooo true . . . even when they get into fights," observed another male teenager from L.A. While there are some racial and ethnic variations, these patterns transcend race and socioeconomic status.

"She found a creative way to use MySpace to check up on her boyfriend by creating a whole new profile, complete with fake pictures, to see if he would cheat on her."

Since new technology can so clearly amplify teens' emotions by shortening the response time and widening the echo chamber, we must realize that one way to help teens deal with their drama is to offer tools to help them slow down, redirect, or tune out using those very same technologies.

"Control" is a word teens use a lot. They want fiercely to be in control of themselves,

---

There are many conflict triggers for teens, but one stands out: Jealousy.

There are many conflict triggers for teens, but one stands out: jealousy. The Teen Relationship Abuse Report states that nearly two-thirds of teens interviewed were with someone who "acted really jealous and asked where they were all of the time." And the ubiquity of communication—online and on mobile phones—amps up the volume on jealous behavior. A segment produced by one of our grantees, Oakland-based Youth Radio, offers these snippets of how online social networks are a jealousy trigger:

"A few months ago, MySpace started some major drama . . . he gave her his password . . . she decided to check up on him, and it led to a surprise . . . he was messaging another girl."

and it is a positive attribute. However, the word "control" also frequently appears in the literature on interpersonal violence, usually in a negative connotation. We need to show that controlling their response to their own emotions—rather than controlling someone else—is the best form of control.

If we do not offer teens ways to control their emotions and to defuse the conflicts that arise in early relationships, then the repercussions will be severe. Early relationship violence is an unfortunate gateway to a whole host of unintended consequences. Not only do young lives spiral out of control, leading to emotional issues, lower graduation rates, incarceration, serious injury, and even death, but the implications on the broader society are also severe. According to the U.S. Centers for Disease Control and Prevention, the national costs of intimate partner violence exceed $5.8 billion each year. The cost of lost productivity alone is almost a billion dollars.

But the real costs are measured in a vicious cycle of damaged lives, as children who witness domestic violence are more than twice as likely to abuse their own partners when they grow up.

Love, acceptance, friendship, self-mastery. These skills and feelings are today, as ever, at the heart of what teens hope to find on their road from childhood to adulthood. But where our road may have been bumpy and potholed, theirs is an information superhighway where affections can be fleeting and heartaches viewed by whole buddy lists. And even though they are living life at full speed and high volume, they still need ways to communicate clearly and dial down the drama.

Crystal Hayling joined Blue Shield of California Foundation as president and CEO in 2004, continuing her longtime commitment to helping under-served communities as a leader of philanthropic organizations. With twenty years of nonprofit and foundation experience, Ms. Hayling has advocated for women, minorities, low-income families, and children through a variety of leadership positions. Prior to joining Blue Shield of California Foundation, Ms. Hayling was senior advisor for the Marguerite Casey Foundation, a Seattle-based foundation committed to helping low-income families strengthen their voice and mobilize their communities to advocate social justice.

Ms. Hayling serves on the boards of Grantmakers in Health and the Center for Effective Philanthropy, and is also a member of the Northern California Advisory Board of College Summit. Ms. Hayling is a 2007 Henry Crown Fellow of the Aspen Institute.

((ACTIONS SPEAK LOUDEST: CONFLICT RESOLUTION

Helping teens understand how to maintain and foster healthy relationships is crucial to their health, safety, and success as adults. Below are some actions that you can begin taking today to help teens cope with the inevitable "drama" in their lives.

IN MY HOME
I CAN . . .

Give teens the tools to defuse conflict.

Right now, teens face a void in dealing with relationship conflicts. Teaching adolescents how to settle immediate or short-term disputes nonviolently will diminish their likelihood of domestic violence in the future. You can direct your teens to Boss of Me (www.BOM411 .com) to give them some of these tools.

Leverage technology as a powerful tool.

A Liz Claiborne study found that a majority of teens and parents believe computers and cell phones make abuse in relationships more likely to occur. While technology can exacerbate teen early relationship conflicts, its organic, fluid presence in the lives of teens also shows its great promise as a medium to make change. We can stay more connected with our teens; we need to better understand the impact that technology has on their relationships to support them and gently guide their usage when necessary.

Teach our children empathy.

From as early an age as possible, help your children put themselves in others' shoes—both for positive and not-so-positive emotions. Encourage your teens to recognize and talk about their feelings, and share your own feelings with them. And remember to empathize with them as well—it may seem trivial to you, but remember that, to a teen, not receiving a call from a girl or boy can be equivalent to not being able to pay the bills.

IN OUR COMMUNITIES
WE SHOULD . . .

Be good role models in our own relationships.

Children and teens take their cues from the people around them. Next time you sense the start of a conflict with someone else or with your own child/teen, take a deep breath and deal with the situation calmly. Teaching your teen that walking away is a strong and admirable solution can be a valuable lesson.

Support groups that support teens.

It is important that our communities address the issue of teen relationships by teaching conflict resolution through school assemblies or workshops, in the classroom, or by encouraging teens to develop peer-to-peer support and training. You can download a Teen Action Tool Kit at the National Center for Victims of Crime (www.ncvc.org) or check out the local offices of the Date Safe Project (www.thedatesafeproject.org) to learn more.

IN OUR COUNTRY
YOU COULD . . .

Donate to organizations that work to reduce teen dating violence.

You can donate to organizations like the Family Violence Prevention Fund (www.endabuse .org), Break the Cycle (www.breakthecycle.org), and Love Is Respect (www.loveisrespect .org), which give teens the skills and tools to develop safe and healthy relationships.

Encourage lawmakers to support programs addressing early relationship conflicts.

Currently, state and local legislation categorizes relationship conflicts as domestic violence, criminalizing the issue and focusing on the back end of the problem. You can encourage lawmakers to address the issue earlier, before the problem escalates.

OUR HOMES

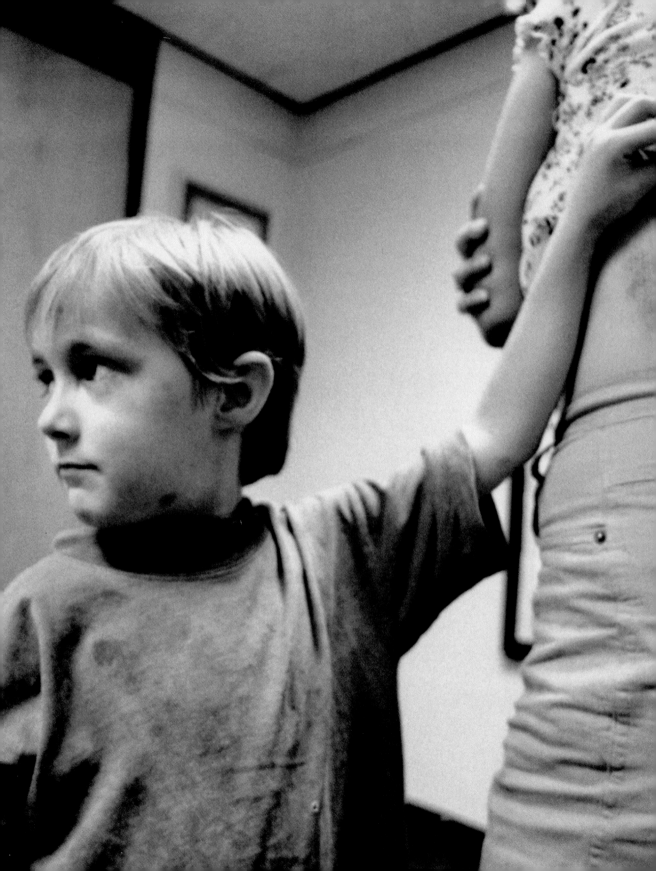

SAFE HOMES))

Joe Torre

JOE TORRE

I grew up in a domestically violent home. I envied people who were raised in a happy household, where their mom and dad got along, and they were hugging all the time, and everything was wonderful.

From the outside, maybe people thought that was true of my family. I was the youngest of five kids, growing up in a middle-class Brooklyn neighborhood. My mom was full of love and support, and my dad was a New York City detective. But when my father was home, it was like walking on eggshells for us all the time. I remember coming home from school and if I saw his car out front, I'd go to a friend's house until it was safe to go home. I connected my dad being there with fear. My dad would yell and bang things and throw food against the wall. What my mom had to endure when he was there is unthinkable. My dad used to come home at night, at maybe 3:00 or 4:00 in the morning, and wake her up to cook for the people he brought home to play cards. And if things weren't done to his liking, there would be hell to pay. I never saw him physically abuse my mom, but I saw evidence that it was taking place. And I later confirmed it with my sisters and brothers, who had stories about my mom being thrown down the staircase.

Most people who aren't exposed to domestic violence are very shocked to find out it goes on in households of every class or race. This is in part maybe because those, like me, who grew up in that kind of environment are embarrassed or ashamed to talk about it. It's not comfortable to discuss or even write about it now. But here I am, a successful person, and I need to let people know that it doesn't always have to be a dirty little secret and that there is more to be gained by talking about it than by staying silent.

To me there's no worse emotion than fear, and when you hear yelling through the walls, it's a helpless feeling. While I was never physically abused, the fear that the emotional abuse created in my life is something I'll never forget. When you grow up always being talked down to, always being told you're not good enough, you get beaten in a different way. Your self-esteem gets beaten down. Your confidence gets beaten out of you. I was a very nervous child. I was very guarded. I used to admire the kids who used to raise their hand, even if it was characterized as a silly question, because they had the courage to ask. I didn't have the courage to even raise my hand in class. I always felt very sensitive about my feelings and was embarrassed to share them with anybody, thinking I was the only one who had these problems. At the time I certainly didn't recognize the connection between domestic violence and my feeling of inadequacy.

A young son shows his mother's bruises to the police. She received the injuries from a fight with her boyfriend. After he threw her behind the couch and choked her, she was able to call the police, have him arrested, and come down to the police station to speak with a family violence counselor. *Viviane Moos/Corbis*

There's nothing more devastating than a climate of abuse and violence at home. A home should be a home, a sanctuary, and a safe harbor from any storm. Yet, for too many children, home is a place of danger and fear of abuse. Studies are now showing just how harmful growing up in this kind of environment can be. Social, emotional, and cognitive development are stunted. Kids fall behind and too many never catch up.

If a child doesn't feel safe at home, it's hard to feel safe anywhere. In this way, I guess I was lucky. I found baseball. I just felt secure playing baseball. I was pretty successful doing it. That was a place I could go hide. A lot of times dur-

lence each year, and millions more are exposed to emotional or verbal abuse. It is just plain sad and unacceptable that in a country like ours we could have so many children growing up in unsafe homes.

Growing up I thought my mom's job was to be there for me. I came home from school, she was there. I came home from playing ball, she was there. There was food on the table, there was a hug, and there was warmness. My mom's name was Margaret. And through our foundation, we created Margaret's Place. There we provide a masters-level counselor, and we provide a safe haven for a child who wants to go into

> When you grow up always being talked down to, always being told you're not good enough, you get beaten in a different way.

ing my childhood I felt I was alone. The Safe at Home Foundation wants kids to know that they are not alone.

When we first started the foundation, we went into a middle school, and I explained that I grew up in this violent home, and that my dad was abusive to my mom. I looked up, and there were probably six or eight youngsters who were just shaking their heads up and down, evidently because they were experiencing the same thing. Six or eight kids in unsafe homes were sitting in just one classroom. It is estimated that over 3.3 million children are exposed to domestic vio-

a room and read a book or play a game. Now I'm very proud to say we have eleven Margaret's Places. But ultimately the answer isn't just more safe havens like these for our children to visit— it's safer homes for them to live in.

A lot of people equate making a lot of money with success. To me success is being able to be there for your children, having them grow up with terrific self-esteem, feeling good about themselves, and being open. I have a young daughter who is thirteen years old. The best thing I can experience with her is to know that she loves coming home every day. Every child should love to come home. And if that's too much too ask, then maybe we should start by making it our societal obligation that at the very least they are not afraid to.

Joe Torre is manager of the Los Angeles Dodgers. He led them to the 2008 division title and their first playoff series win in twenty years. Torre spent the previous twelve seasons as manager of the New York Yankees. The Yankees made the playoffs every year under his tenure, and he led them to six World Series appearances during the twelve-year span, winning four World Series Championships.

Torre is a three-time AP Manager of the Year Award winner and in 1996 was named Sportsman of the Year by the *Sporting News*. During his seventeen-year playing career, Torre was a nine-time All-Star, a Gold Glove–winning catcher, and was the National League's Most Valuable Player in 1971.

He is the co-author of three books: *Chasing the Dream: My Lifelong Journey to the World Series; Joe Torre's Ground Rules for Winners: 12 Keys to Managing Team Players, Tough Bosses, Setbacks, and Success;* and *The Yankee Years.*

In 2002, Torre and his wife, Ali, launched the Joe Torre Safe at Home Foundation, whose mission is educating to end the cycle of domestic violence and save lives.

((ACTIONS SPEAK LOUDEST: SAFE HOMES

It is estimated that 3.3 million children are exposed to domestic abuse each year. What is not known is how many more children dread going home because of the stress and fear associated with what should be a safe environment. This experience does more than scar; it normalizes abuse and turns a place children should regard as their refuge into a place filled with anxiety. Here's how you can help kids feel safe at home.

IN MY HOME
I CAN . . .

Provide a safe home environment for children and myself.

Studies show that children exposed to long-term domestic abuse are likely to suffer from post-traumatic stress disorder and suffer developmentally. It's about more than hitting, it's about stress and behavior—such as yelling and put-downs—that is inhibitive of healthy, happy development. Avoid turning your stress into theirs.

Educate children on the importance of respect for others and healthy emotional expression.

When adults take an active role in educating children to express their frustration in a constructive manner and teach them to respect each other, they are less likely to become abusive adults themselves. For more information you can visit www.endabuse.org or www.menagainstdv.org.

Encourage children to be assertive and maintain a positive self-regard.

Kids vested with a greater sense of self-worth and equipped with the tools to assert themselves will be less likely to be in abusive relationships as they get older. Nurture their interests and support the pursuit of specific goals through activities such as sports or the arts that encourage self-esteem and promote positive self-image.

IN OUR COMMUNITIES
WE SHOULD . . .

Speak up when we witness potential indicators of abuse.

The shame and anxiety children attach to living in an abusive environment make it difficult for children to express their feelings or confide in anyone, much less access the help they may need. When we witness abuse, or a child confides in us, we have a responsibility to speak for them. Contact local authorities or visit www.childhelp.org for assistance and resources.

Get involved in a safe outlet.

Help provide healthy, safe settings for kids. Volunteer your time by coaching in a local youth league or volunteering at a local community organization like the Boys & Girls Club. For more information visit www.dosomething.org or www.bgca.org.

IN OUR COUNTRY
YOU COULD . . .

Petition our legislators to take stronger stances on domestic violence.

In 2005 *Mother Jones* reported that domestic abuse programs were underfunded by $48 million. While there are programs that respond to domestic violence, there are relatively few programs that focus on the prevention of initial incidents, such as the CDC's DELTA Program, The Family Violence Prevention Fund, or the Blue Shield of California Foundation. More funding needs to be directed to these programs so that abuse is addressed before it becomes chronic.

Support Joe Torre's Safe at Home Foundation.

Margaret's Place, started by the Safe at Home Foundation, has several locations around the country for kids living in abusive situations to seek free counseling, do homework, or just find refuge. Visit www.joetorre.org for more information.

CHARACTER))

Joe Paterno

JOE PATERNO

It is an era of text messages, cell phones, the Internet, mind-numbing video games, and hundreds of television channels. I don't understand the need for all of them or even how they work. I do know that they make the process of maturing into a responsible and contributing adult much more difficult by their presence. And that's not just true for the 2,500-plus football players I have coached since starting my career at Penn State in 1950, but for all of today's kids.

As a coach, my primary responsibilities are to mold my players into good citizens, develop their character, help them be good students, and teach them to be successful. Those responsibilities are the same challenges for all coaches, teachers, and parents. It is a daunting task, given all the distractions and temptations that kids face today, but nothing is more worthwhile and fulfilling.

Today's gadgets and electronics do nothing to test true mettle or build morals. They erase personal relationships and accountability. And they engender the mistaken belief that problems can be solved by flipping a switch or pounding a button.

While at Penn State, we have been fortunate to have won two national championships, and we've had five undefeated seasons. Over the

During the 2007 football season, after just a few players were cited for disciplinary issues, Coach Joe Paterno decided to hold the entire team accountable. As a result, all of his players were required to help clean up Beaver Stadium after their home games. Seating capacity for the stadium is almost 110,000. *Courtesy of Steve Manuel*

years, our kids—like all young people—have faced obstacles and challenges, some external and some internal. Most of the time, as players and as people, our kids rose above these events. The point is, there will always be hurdles and challenges that test your character. It is our responsibility to show today's youth the right direction.

When times are difficult, we—as teachers, parents, coaches—must be at our absolute best. That is when today's kids really pay atten-

had been defeated and destroyed—his army waged war and endured hell, year after year. They suffered storms and shipwrecks and pestilence, terrible elements they couldn't control while fighting battles they tried to control. What has made that drama last for two thousand years is not the temporary wins and losses, but the courage and the determination to endure, rising above the tricks and treacheries of fate to survive and create a new city.

> There will always be hurdles and challenges that test your character. It is our responsibility to show today's youth the right direction.

tion. That's when a parent or teacher matters the most. As Martin Luther King Jr. said, "The ultimate measure of a man is not where he stands in moments of comfort and convenience, but where he stands at times of challenge and controversy."

These are lessons for us all. You can't coast. You need to constantly take care of the little things the right way, and the big things will take care of themselves. It is a process that will stand our youth in good stead for the future. If they succeed in the face of failure, they will know of what they are made. Emerson never buckled a chinstrap, but he knew what he was talking about when he wrote, "What lies behind us and what lies before us are small matters compared to what lies within us."

Success to me is not all about winning a game. When Aeneas left his city of Troy—which

Inevitably, as much as we try to direct them, kids take a misstep or two, in a variety of ways for a variety of reasons. I still believe they should be disciplined, something that every child, student, and athlete deserves. We look at players as individuals, and at their circumstances as unique. And we try to tailor our response yet still hold them accountable. These are kids—eighteen, nineteen, twenty years old—we are talking about. They are going to mess up. Former president Jimmy Carter had it right, I think, when he said, "To deal with individual human needs at the everyday level can be noble sometimes."

Of course, a team is a living, breathing organism with responsibilities for the entire unit, to be on a singular course and to be responsible for all of its members. Brotherhood. And that's true of our teams at Penn State. The coaches preach and teach, but it is the players who must look out for each other, to serve as a moral compass and to give a kick in the pants for those who are losing their way.

Now more than ever, we need to keep our priorities in line. We need to tell kids, "Don't let the world pass you by. Go after life. Attack it." The challenges that are met and conquered in the classroom, on the playing fields, in the library, and in the community are real. They build character. The challenges met by a video screen are artificial and only test manual dexterity.

A Catholic theologian who is kind of a hero of mine, Mike Novak, writes extensively on sports and theology. The following is from his book *The Joy of Sports:*

I believe that sports are not merely entertainment, but are rooted in necessities and aspirations of the human spirit. They provide an ennobling quality, a joy that can lift us out of our own lives and put us in touch with the highest standards of excellence. They can inspire us to stretch our bodies and our spirits. Sports must be treated with all the intelligence and care and love that the human spirit can bring to bear. Sports at their heart are a special kind of reality, a spiritual activity, a kind of naturalistic religion, a tribute to grace and beauty and excellence. Sports help the athlete and spectator alike to keep the streams of the spirit running clean and strong.

Art and music and literature and philosophy and religion add to the quality of our lives. Without them, we'd have trouble knowing where we came from. We'd have trouble expressing ourselves across generations. They help us understand our humanity. And so does sport.

Educators, on and off the playing field, and parents, deal with the most important issues in life, like commitment, discipline, loyalty, pride, and character. These are the things that make a difference in this country and make a difference for a lifetime.

For fifty-nine years and 669 games through the 2008 college football season, Joe Paterno has passionately served the Penn State football program and his university with principle, distinction, and success with honor. The 2008 season was Joe Paterno's forty-third as head coach of the Nittany Lions, continuing an unprecedented stretch in American sports. In December 2007, Paterno was inducted into the National Football Foundation and College Football Hall of Fame. He is widely regarded as the most successful coach in the history of college football, on and off the field.

Gifts from Joe and wife Sue have endowed faculty positions and scholarships in the College of the Liberal Arts; the School of Architecture and Landscape Architecture; and supported the University Libraries (where a wing is named after his family).

((ACTIONS SPEAK LOUDEST: CHARACTER

Eleanor Roosevelt sagely contended that "people grow through experience if they meet life honestly and courageously. This is how character is built." Each moment of a child's life stamps its essence upon their developing character, and how they react and handle these experiences defines who they will become. Below you will find resources to encourage character development in the lives of your child and all children.

IN MY HOME
I CAN . . .

Establish responsibility as a family obligation early on.

You should set up expectations for your child's individual responsibilities at home through a weekly chore list or daily homework time. Encouraging your children to keep their promises and rewarding them for being trustworthy creates a model for accountability they can build upon. As a parent, the same is true: If you promise your children a treat, a consequence, a vacation, or special time together, then do it.

Let my children practice losing as well as winning.

Young children relish defeating their parents at simple card and board games, but always winning these games at home may set up unrealistic expectations for when they play with their friends, and can encourage them to develop a tendency for inflexibility. Be fair. Share the love of playing the game rather than emphasizing the outcome.

Embrace discipline as a device to shape my child's development.

Establish and maintain limits in the child's psychological, social, and physical environments by monitoring their pursuits and influences. It is important for children to recognize that their actions have consequences. The American Academy of Pediatrics offers advice regarding how to discipline your child in a section dedicated to children's health topics on their Web site (www.aap.org/healthtopics).

IN OUR COMMUNITIES
WE SHOULD . . .

Encourage our children to work summer jobs as babysitters or lifeguards.
Employment that combines responsibility for others and citizenship endows children with
a sense of self-esteem that is unparalleled. The American Red Cross provides training
courses to prepare interested youth in these services.

Demonstrate compassion by supporting local initiatives for those in need.
Many volunteer opportunities can be found online through www.idealist.org or www.volunteer
match.org. You might also want to think about what charitable acts you can do for others
as a family, including spending a day visiting with seniors in a nursing home or having a
lemonade stand or bake sale with the proceeds going toward a nonprofit of your child's
choosing.

IN OUR COUNTRY
YOU COULD . . .

Join the national Character Counts! Coalition.
The Josephson Institute Center for Sports Ethics developed this coalition, and their site
is a wonderful resource for teachers, parents, and coaches seeking the tools to develop a
child's character (http://josephsoninstitute.org/sports). Membership in the coalition provides access to various materials that allow you to integrate this flexible methodology into
your school or organization.

MORAL INTELLIGENCE))

Robert Coles

ROBERT COLES

A child is shaped at the very start of life by the values of certain adults. Even before a boy or girl is born, his or her parents are already giving expression to their values in a way that will matter for their son or daughter. A woman tries to think of others, not only of herself—and so she watches what she eats and drinks, stays away from cigarettes, establishes regular contact with an obstetrician, not only out of concern for herself but with her future child in mind. A man takes an interest in the woman who is carrying his child as well as hers, visits the doctor with her, offers her comfort, reassurance, and affection as someone himself deeply involved in an important event: A pregnancy is ideally two people concerned about a third person soon to arrive. This attitude of caring, lived out daily, has direct consequences for that growing fetus: the earliest time in its life when the Golden Rule will decisively affect its life.

To be sure, many women and men who are soon to become parents don't give explicit or continuing thought to the moral significances of their attentive concern for their future child. Rather, they are simply being sensible, natural. Yet all too many women and men who are responsible for a pregnancy don't act responsibly, don't take what's best for the other, the child, into account and act accordingly. The result is an unborn child already at risk—there is a distinct possibility of physical harm from the mother's use of alcohol, drugs, or cigarettes, or from disease, and a likelihood of psychological vulnerability that can arise when parents show from the start that they are unlikely to value the child enough to behave in a way that will make a difference down the line.

It is one thing to lay claim to values and quite another to try and live them out, enact them over time in connection with others.

"Good children" are boys and girls who in the first place have learned to take seriously that very notion, the desirability of goodness, a living up to the Golden Rule, a respect for others, a commitment of mind, heart, soul to one's family, neighborhood, and nation—and have also learned that the issue of goodness is not an abstract one, but rather a concrete expressive one: how to turn the rhetoric of goodness into action, moments that affirm the presence of goodness in a particular lived life.

The task for each of us, I suspect, is to try to learn not only what we want for our children morally, but also what we don't want. No question, some of our young are most certainly caught in a moral undertow, headed nowhere fast. We have all confronted certain quite harmful children, children who are already not so

Ruby Nell Bridges at age six was the first African-American child to attend William Franz Elementary School in New Orleans after courts ordered the desegregation of public schools. Her remarkable moral intelligence was featured in books by Dr. Robert Coles and was embodied in her constant consideration and empathy for those who were against desegregation. *Courtesy of the Corbis Bettmann Collection* good, going on bad; children who are impulsive, demanding, insensitive, wrapped up in themselves to the point that others mean very little.

Our sons and daughters, our students of whatever age, are on the lookout for moral direction. Babies need to learn no and yes. Elementary school children need to learn how to get along with others, how to engage with them in the tradition of the Golden Rule as one would hope to be engaged by them. Teenagers need to figure out how to regard their newly capable, yearning bodies as well as the various interests and preferences and attitudes constantly being thrust upon them by friends, by advertisements,

notion of how one ought to behave under a variety of circumstances. Much of all that—the day-to-day encounters with children, during which we say yes or no, smile or frown, advocate one or another line of thought, course of action—is done quite naturally, by "instinct," that is, with no great amount of deliberative energy extended. We possess in our hearts, our bones, our guts (wherever our particular anatomy of moral intuition would locate it), an ethical sense of things, and we draw on it constantly. We also know way down within ourselves how eagerly most children look for moral clues from their parents, their teachers.

> A child is shaped at the very start of life by the values of certain adults.

by actors and actresses, announcers, singers and musicians, by sports heroes. How can we—you and I, as parents or as teachers—do the best possible job of handing our principles and convictions and values to this next generation, which belongs to our children or students?

No question, some of us don't really stop and think about such a challenge until some trouble arrives at our door—then comes the moral alarm and anxiety: what to say, what to do. We may forget that, prior to that particular time of crisis or concern, we have all along been making certain moral points to our children, sending them messages directly or by implication; in their sum, our

I have a story of my own son going to a hospital. One day I was sitting at my desk writing when he came into my study, bleeding. He'd done what he was told not to do; he'd gotten some of the tools in the barn and used them and cut himself badly. Although he had not severed an artery, I had to get him to the hospital. I felt that he ought to get there fast, so I was speeding. I was going through red lights, and frankly splashing some people because it was a rain-drenched day.

My son turned to me and he said, "Dad, to get out of trouble we're going to make more trouble." He really gave me a moral moment there, and a lesson. I slowed down and thought, "I am learning something from this nine-year-old boy that I know he's learned from his mother about moral behavior. I am a student and he is a teacher."

 **Robert Coles** is a professor of psychiatry and medical humanities at Harvard Medical School and a research psychiatrist for Harvard University Health Services. His many books include the Pulitzer Prize–winning five-volume *Children of Crisis*, *The Moral Intelligence of Children*, and *The Spiritual Intelligence of Children*. Coles's accomplishments have earned him the Pulitzer Prize for General Nonfiction (1973), a MacArthur Award (1981), the Presidential Medal of Freedom (1998), and the National Humanities Medal (2001).

He has written over seventy-five books, writes regular columns in the *New Republic*, *New Oxford Review*, and *American Poetry Review*, and co-founded the magazine *DoubleTake*. Coles is also the James Agee Professor of Social Ethics at Harvard.

((ACTIONS SPEAK LOUDEST: MORAL INTELLIGENCE

One might say that a child's moral upbringing serves as the foundation for their life; how they will treat others, shape their careers, and ultimately, effect change, can be directly correlated to their moral nature. It is important to recognize that each child seeks guidance as they build this foundation. Albert Einstein said, "Setting an example is not the main means of influencing another, it is the only means."

IN MY HOME
I CAN . . .

Be present.
Parental absence allows a variety of moral influences to permeate the home. By simply being there with your child as much as possible, you can effectively work to combat negative influences.

Set a good example.
Children learn moral intelligence from the outside world; their greatest influence is your own behavior. Remember that they are always watching, listening, and learning from your actions.

Expose my children to books and films with moral lessons.
Many great works of children's literature house moral lessons, such as *Aesop's Fables*, *The Giving Tree*, *Charlotte's Web*, and *The Velveteen Rabbit*. Additionally, there are many children's films that can bring ethics into your home, including *E.T.*, *To Kill a Mockingbird*, *The Wizard of Oz*, and *Pay It Forward*. These instructive stories bring to light issues children can grasp in a setting designed for them.

IN OUR COMMUNITIES
WE SHOULD . . .

Encourage our schools to integrate moral intelligence into the curriculum.
School-age children begin the journey of moral development as their interest grows in how and why the world works as it does. Therefore, developing a curriculum that includes moral teaching gives confidence and structure to children to grow as moral thinkers outside the home. The National Education Association has a great resource on their Web site called "Do the Right Thing" with advice and materials for educators seeking to promote respectful student behavior (www.nea.org/tools/3153.htm).

Create a parenting book club around the works of Dr. Robert Coles.
Dr. Coles's commitment to analyzing the moral and spiritual life of children provides rich fodder for discussion, and the book club, by extension, creates a space where parents can talk to others about the challenges raising moral children brings.

Volunteer with children at a shelter or place of worship.
In order to establish our commitment to making the world a better place and helping those less fortunate than us, community service offers us all a chance to think about those we seek to help not only abstractly, but also concretely.

IN OUR COUNTRY
YOU COULD . . .

Discover the Foundation for a Better Life.
An organization dedicated to sharing the values that make a difference in our communities, they have created public service campaigns that model the benefits of a life lived by principles. In turn, they hope to inspire people to make values a part of their own lives, and then to communicate the benefits to others: www.values.com.

metabolic rate that is actually lower than sleeping. No wonder we have an obesity issue.

Some may say it is just media and there are more important issues regarding our children to worry about. But as scholar Marie Winn noted, scratch any issue concerning kids today (obesity, education, violence, apathy) and you won't have to dig too far to find the influence of media. When we choose to talk about the issue of children and the media, we go to the content. Are video games too violent? Are hip-hop lyrics too suggestive? These questions are easier. We can wrap our heads around them. We can even control them. But what of the bigger question, the watching television? Fractured sentences, distracted thoughts, entire meals that pass with little communication. Sad, considering that when parents spend just one hour a day talking to their children, we see significant increases in academic performance.

And what about their imagination, or lack thereof? Making up games or writing and telling stories born from the fertile mind of childhood are lost arts. Electronic media is a very literal exercise; it is taken at face value. Imagination need not apply.

When we first met Matthew, the boy in the picture, it was 3:00 p.m. on a sunny day and he

> In the virtual world of television and video games, there is always a happy ending.

more difficult and neglected one? Is it all too much? Televisions are in every bedroom, DVDs in the minivan, music videos and movies on cell phones, every form of media is at their fingertips twenty-four/seven. And it may not be a matter of what is happening when one watches but what does not happen during all those hours in front of screens; the hours not spent playing outside, using their imaginations, the conversations never had, the activities never tried.

Think about the home. There is no more living in the living room. Just watching. In the dining room, where conversation used to flow, many meals are now served with a side of television. Have you ever watched a family eat while was already in his pajamas, inside for the day. In his small, two-bedroom apartment, you will find three television sets, three video game systems, two DVD players, and a VHS. He prefers video games and television to everything else, including going outside to play. He owns sixty video games. He has watched his current favorite movie, *The Incredibles*, over twenty times. He spends more than forty hours a week in front of a screen. He recently quit baseball because it's too hard to play compared to video games. He is your average seven-year-old boy.

Like the majority of children, he is spending too much of his early life watching and not enough of it living, too much time observing the adult world through media instead of directly interacting with the world around him with a sense of wonder and curiosity that is the essence of childhood. Finally, if you need one more number to tell this story, try this one on. By the time Matthew turns thirty, he will have spent almost ten years, one whole decade of his life, dedicated to one activity—consuming media.

 **Robert McKinnon** is founder and president of YELLOWBRICK-ROAD, a company that designs social change through programming, communications, advocacy, and action.

YELLOWBRICKROAD works on issues ranging from childhood obesity to climate change. He is proud to have partnered with change makers within the U.S. Department of Health and Human Services, the International Olympic Committee, National Geographic, The Boys' Club of New York, the Robert Wood Johnson Foundation, and many other organizations to help millions of Americans overcome obstacles on their way to a healthier and happier life.

Among others, the Institute of Medicine, the National Institute of Health, the Federal Trade Commission, the National Governors Association, and the U.S. Congress, have called upon McKinnon to provide honest perspective on the many issues facing us today. He has appeared on NPR's *All Things Considered* and has been interviewed by the *Wall Street Journal, Washington Post,* and other media outlets to comment on issues facing our country.

He is also the creator and editor of this collection.

(((ACTIONS SPEAK LOUDEST: SCREEN TIME

As a parent, community member, and citizen there is much you can do to ensure that our children grow up living their own lives and not watching others. Below are some simple actions that you can start taking today to make a difference.

IN MY HOME
I CAN . . .

Watch how much they watch.
The American Academy of Pediatrics recommends that no children under the age of two watch any television and that those over that age limit their screen time to no more than two hours a day.

Create a responsible home media environment.
A recent Kaiser Family Foundation study suggests that simply removing televisions and video games from a child's room will decrease children's screen time by over an hour a day.

Set clear, simple rules for family media consumption.
The Kaiser study showed that those parents who set some simple rules as to when and how much time their children spent with media also saw an hour reduction in consumption. Visit www .kff.org for their suggestions.

IN OUR COMMUNITIES
WE SHOULD . . .

Encourage our schools to adopt media literacy programs.

Fewer than 10 percent of schools teach media literacy, meaning that our children have few tools to understand the media choices they make and the messages they see. Check out the Center for Media Literacy for more information on the benefits of media literacy (www.medialit.org).

Engage our entire families and neighborhoods.

Annual events such as TV Turnoff Week (www.turnoffyourtv.com) and Family Dinner Day (www.casafamilyday.org) offer opportunities for families to explore the benefits of spending time together without media. Studies have shown that spending just an hour a day talking to your children can result in improved academic performance and lower incidences of negative behaviors such as drug use.

Support community organizations that give kids alternatives.

Organizations such as the YMCA (www.ymca.net), Boy Scouts (www.scouting.org), and Girl Scouts (www.girlscouts.org) provide exciting alternatives for children to engage and learn key skills versus watching.

IN OUR COUNTRY
YOU COULD . . .

Join advocacy groups that share your concerns.

Groups such as Children Now (www.childrennow.org), Common Sense Media (www.commonsensemedia.org), and the Kaiser Family Foundation (www.kff.org) are valuable resources and advocates for our children on media-related issues. See how you can be involved in their important efforts.

Talk to the FCC and your elected officials.

On March 21, 2007, the Children and Media Research Act was introduced. The bill would facilitate research into the effects of media on children. It is currently still under consideration. Go to www.senate.gov, www.house.gov, or www.fcc.gov to find out how you can reach your congressman and senators to express your support for issues such as these.

Studies show children are spending less time playing creatively. This may not sound like much of a loss, but play is the foundation of divergent thinking, school success, constructive problem solving, and something more fundamentally human—the capacity to delight in our own creations and make life meaningful. Make believe can design the future, reshape the past, engender new possibilities, and embody powerful feelings. If allowed to flourish, it's how children naturally reflect on their experience and make sense of it—enabling a sense of mastery over confusing, troubling, or overwhelming events.

True creative play is as individual as fingerprints. None of us experience the world in exactly

Lovable media characters, cutting-edge technology, brightly colored packaging, and well-funded, psychologically savvy marketing strategies combine in coordinated campaigns to capture the hearts, minds, and imaginations of children—teaching them to value that which can be bought over their own make believe creations.

Children today are spending more time with electronic media than any activity other than sleeping—and most of it is commercially based. Forty percent of three-month-old babies regularly "watch" television and DVDs for an average of forty-five minutes a day. And 19 percent of babies under the age of one have a TV set in their bedroom. Web-based social networking sites and

True creative play is as individual as fingerprints.

the same way and our differences emerge in our creations. When children get to slay their own particular monsters, become a rescue worker in a hurricane, or take the role of an exasperated parent, they bring to light dreams, fantasies, and fears that can be examined and conquered.

Play is so fundamental to children's health and well-being—and so endangered—that the United Nations lists it as a guaranteed right in its Convention on the Rights of the Child. For children in the Third World, societal horrors such as exploitation through slavery, child conscription, and child labor deny children their right to play. In the United States and other industrialized nations, seduction, not conscription, lures children away from creative play.

virtual worlds like Webkinz, Club Penguin, and Barbiegirl are targeting five-year-olds, and one called Knowledge Adventure is being marketed to children as young as three. Screens in the backseats of minivans, in cell phones, and on portable DVD players—to say nothing of restaurants and pediatricians' offices—mean that many children are exposed to screen media and the products they market almost all of their waking hours. The time, space, and silence available for their own ideas and their own images, for creative play, for unhurried interactions with people, for reading, or being read to, shrinks with every blockbuster children's film or television program (inevitably accompanied by a flood of "tie-in" foods, toys, books, videos, and clothing). In addition, the toys most heavily marketed to children are those that actually undermine creative play—toys like the Tickle Me Elmo series, which are linked to media and/or require nothing from a child but the push of a button in order to move, speak, or play music.

A child immersed in a commercialized, electronic world has no experience of generating her own fun or creating her own world. She's in constant need of external stimulation and a sitting duck for marketing designed to convince her that only the latest widget will relieve her boredom, and she takes pleasure solely from the things corporations sell. In a market-driven society, creative play is a bust. It just isn't lucrative. The satisfactions gleaned from make believe depend more on the person playing than on what's purchased to play with.

Children who play creatively find multiple uses for objects. They transform a blanket into a tent one day and a cave the next. A stick becomes a magic wand, a sword, a flagpole, and a mast for a schooner. The toys that nurture imagination—blocks, art supplies, dolls, and stuffed animals free of computer chips and links to media—can be used repeatedly and in a variety of ways. When it comes to make believe, less really is more.

In a world where glitz masquerades for substance and pundits tout technology as a panacea, it's tempting to shower even babies and toddlers with the latest electronic wonders—but it's a disaster for make believe. While pushing techno toys on infants who aren't even asking for them is a boon to big business, it means we can no longer assume that young children even know how to play.

We're not at the point of surgically inserting microchips in babies' brains. But when we succumb to marketing hype about electronic toddler toys, we raise a generation of children in thrall to corporations for stimulation and soothing, who will never know the value of their own visions, or the exquisite pleasure of creating voices that no one else can hear.

Psychologist Susan Linn is associate director of the media center of the Judge Baker Children's Center, instructor in psychiatry at Harvard Medical School, and director of the Campaign for a Commercial-Free Childhood. Her books, *Consuming Kids: The Hostile Takeover of Childhood* and *The Case for Make Believe: Saving Play in a Commercialized World* have been praised in publications as diverse as the *Wall Street Journal*, the *Boston Globe*, and *Mother Jones*. Dr. Linn is an internationally recognized expert on play and the impact of commercialism on children and has appeared on such national media programs as *60 Minutes, NOW with Bill Moyers, Good Morning America*, and *World News Tonight*.

In 2006 Dr. Linn was awarded a Presidential Citation from the American Psychological Association for her work on behalf of children.

(((ACTIONS SPEAK LOUDEST: MAKE BELIEVE

An estimated $600 billion is spent on youth-targeted marketing. With the nearly infinite reach of media through the Internet, and the constant barrage of images that children are subjected to on a daily basis, there is an ever-diminishing space for imagination in an ever-increasing digital world. Below are a variety of ways to guard against consumer culture and ensure the robust development of one of the most valuable resources children have at their disposal—their imagination.

IN MY HOME
I CAN . . .

Make believe with a child.
You can encourage a child to be more creative by making believe together. Do something fun like make a puppet show together or create a game. For some ideas visit www.creativekidsathome.com/activities.shtml.

Limit exposure to marketing.
There is a wellspring of children-targeted Web sites that are affiliated with specific channels, products, and other media. Monitor children's Internet usage and dissuade them from using sites that are simply an extension of the commercials they see on television.

Avoid purchasing products with direct merchandising ties.
Many children's products on the market are part of a larger merchandising strategy with books and toys tied to movies and video games. When a product is a stand-in for an existing character, children rely less on their own creativity for the narratives that accompany play. Try to make purchases that don't always reinforce a prescribed brand or market a new movie.

IN OUR COMMUNITIES
WE SHOULD . . .

Demand responsible use of advertising.
Corporations have recently taken to "grassroots" marketing, namely partnering with schools, churches, and even hospitals to "reach target audiences where they live, work, and play." Push community leaders and local politicians to acknowledge the value of commercial-free neighborhoods.

Communicate media literacy with children.
It has been demonstrated that very young children cannot discern between advertising and programming, and children up until the age of eight have difficulty understanding that the aim of advertising is to persuade consumers to purchase products. Adults should talk about advertising and programming with kids.

Support arts education.
The decline of arts education combined with marketing-saturated media has dire consequences for the development of creativity or imagination, and consequently for the development of interpretive and critical tools necessary for bright, engaged citizens. We run the risk of creating a public sphere peopled with consumers first and thinkers second.

IN OUR COUNTRY
YOU COULD . . .

Ask our public officials to demand greater corporate responsibility.
Marketing of educational products is often inaccurate and counters expert opinion about the role digital and visual media should play in a young child's development (the consensus typically being little to none). Contact the Federal Trade Commission Bureau of Consumer Protection to demand more responsible practices (877-FTC-HELP or www.ftc .gov/ftc/contact.shtm).

Support national initiatives to limit advertising in certain public spaces.
Visit the Campaign for a Commercial-Free Childhood (www.commercialexploitation.org/ campaigns.htm) for information on what measures you can take to stop advertisers from targeting children in school and other inappropriate spaces.

whom they serve, but also on the communities where we all live.

Not surprisingly, science is revealing a number of tangible benefits that come from connecting youth to their elders. A report from the U.S. Environmental Protection Agency Aging Institute on the benefits of intergenerational programs found that, for youth, these programs enhance social skills by improving communications skills, promoting self-esteem, and developing problem-solving abilities. Youth involved in

A study from the Harvard School of Public Health found social engagement could have as much effect on prolonging life as fitness activities. Keeping social and busy evokes changes in the brain that protect against cognitive decline. This, in turn, influences physical processes regulated by the brain such as cellular immunity or mobilizing the body's defenses against disease.

And finally, several sources have found that intergenerational programs are a cost-efficient means of addressing community issues. Ulti-

> We need to create a seismic change in how we view and treat our relationship to our elders.

these programs are almost one-third less likely to hit others. In addition, youth involved in intergenerational programs are 46 percent less likely to initiate drug use, and among minorities that number increases to 70 percent.

A study from the Corporation for National Service in Washington concluded that older adults had a measurable impact on students' reading performance, attitudes about reading, self-confidence, and motivation to read. The author of the research stated, "Something unique stems from the nature of the intergenerational relationship. The dynamic of that relationship—reciprocal and accepting—gives rise to opportunities for learning, growth, and understanding for both participants."

mately they tend to unite community members to take action on public policy issues that address human needs across generations. Also, they often achieve efficiencies by sharing human and financial resources.

There are clear economic, social, and health benefits to bringing our elders and youth together. But if the above isn't convincing, then consider this when thinking about this connection: We are who they were—and they are who we will become. It is in our collective self-interest to create these connections. Creating more caring children, who empathize with the situations of our elders, means we will be creating more responsible adults who will be caring for us one day.

It is important now—not later, but now—to create a profound shift in attitudes toward the value of creating stronger relationships between our young and our elderly. We need to create a seismic change in how we view and treat our relationship to our elders: to learn from the wisdom and life lessons they have to teach us and to give them the dignity and respect they are due by caring for them in a more interactive way. Concurrently, children are given an opportunity to develop a moral compass for themselves and inspire a sense of personal responsibility carried through life.

Like the elephants, many of the issues facing our children could be mitigated by stronger connections with the experiences of our elders.

Imagine in Mississippi, a twelve-year-old son of a single mother comes to understand freedom through the eyes of a 115-year-old daughter of a former slave. In New York, a sixteen-year-old dancer is inspired to perform by a ninety-year-old Ziegfeld girl. In San Jose, an orphan appreciates family by connecting with a band of brothers from World War II. Imagine, any one of our youth today coping better in troubling economic times by listening to an eighty-seven-year-old woman who as a child herself lived through the Great Depression. Imagine if the deadening crackling of digital snow were replaced with a million connections like these, between the youngest and eldest among us.

Jerry Friedman, award-winning photographer, author, speaker, and founder of Earth's Elders, has spent the past four years on a landmark project to introduce the world to the sixty oldest people on earth. Through his globe-trotting journey to document their lives, Friedman has become a leading expert on supercentenarians, those who have lived 110 years or more. No one else in history has ever met so many of the oldest people on earth.

Earth's Elders was recognized with a month-long show at the United Nations, the Capitol Rotunda in Washington, and in Tokyo. The foundation's current goal is to help make one million connections between our oldest and youngest citizens.

(((ACTIONS SPEAK LOUDEST: ELDER CONNECTIONS

Intergenerational connections are a significant part of a successful and thriving country. It is through these connections that individual lives and communities can be strengthened. Below are some suggestions—inspired by youngsters and elders alike—to help improve quality of life through the sharing of lives.

IN MY HOME
I CAN . . .

Connect a child with an elder.
Studies show, and history has proven, the importance of creating strong connections between our youngest and oldest. Social engagement positively impacts mental, physical, and cognitive health. You can teach children the value of these connections and provide opportunities for them to get together with their grandparents or elders. Encourage children to visit with their elders regularly, share experiences, make weekly phone calls, and send letters or e-mails.

Share pictures and stories.
Take pictures with your children and their favorite elders. Children can then send pictures to elders to brighten their day and share stories with them about what they're working on in school and with their friends. Children and elders can also connect by sending an online postcard at www.earthselders.org/shareyourstory.php or by posting photos online to share with friends and family.

IN OUR COMMUNITIES
WE SHOULD . . .

Connect a school with a local nursing home.

Start a program at a local school to visit nursing homes in your community (or vice versa—start a program that gets elders on the move visiting schools). A regular group visit can go a long way and keep elders mentally fit, happy, and healthy and youth eager to learn more through a living history. Creating more caring children, who empathize with the situation of our elders, means we will be creating more responsible adults who will be caring for us one day. There are many suggestions and resources listed at Generations United (www.gu.org), a national organization that brings youth and elders together through various programs around the country.

Implement a school-based program.

Work with your local school system to implement a program to increase students' awareness and positive attitudes toward the elderly. Earth's Elders and Bank Street College put together a curriculum (and teachers' guide) that focuses on the literary genre of biography and has been designed as a unit of study that can fit into the ongoing literacy curriculum (www.earthselders.org/connect_educator.php).

Encourage elders to volunteer or mentor at a local school.

Volunteering gives elders meaningful ways to be socially active and builds their support group. When elders volunteer, they show increased physical and mental capabilities—studies show it can help fend off dementia. Students in turn benefit from having a mentor by getting better test scores and showing better overall behavior. For more information on how to participate, refer to Experience Corps, www.experiencecorps.org/in.

IN OUR COUNTRY
YOU COULD . . .

Support organizations that advocate for elder issues and promote intergenerational connections.

A donation—of your time or money—to Earth's Elders (www.earthselders.org) or the AARP (www.aarp.org/issues/dividedwefail/get_involved/) can help in many different ways, from advancing intergenerational-based school curriculum to advocating for financial security and affordable health care for future generations.

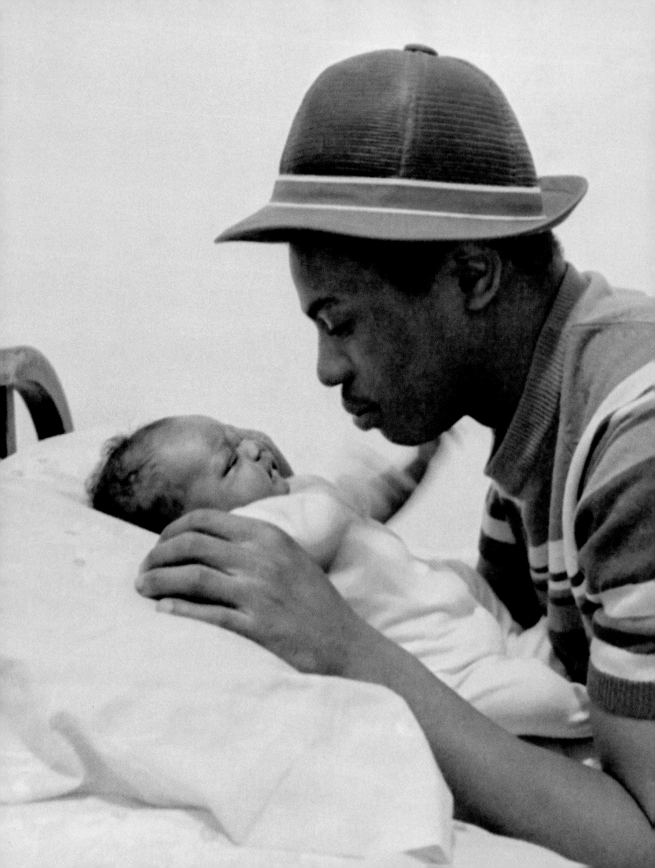

FATHERHOOD 🔊

JUAN WILLIAMS

Walter Dean Myers, a best-selling author of books for teenagers, sometimes visits juvenile detention centers in his home state of New Jersey to hold writing workshops and listen for stories about the lives of young Americans.

One day, in a juvenile facility near his home in Jersey City, a fifteen-year-old black boy pulled him aside for a whispered question: Why did he write in *Somewhere in the Darkness* about a boy not meeting his father because the father was in jail? Mr. Myers, a seventy-year-old black man, did not answer. He waited. And sure enough, the boy, eyes down, mumbled that he had yet to meet his own father, who was in jail.

Each year we celebrate Father's Day, but seldom reflect upon a sad fact: It is now common to meet young people in our big-city schools, foster-care homes, and juvenile centers who do not know their dads. Most of those children have come face-to-face with their father at some point, but most have little regular contact with the man, or do not have any faith that he loves or cares about them.

When fatherless young people are encouraged to write about their lives, they tell heartbreaking stories about feeling like "throwaway people." In the privacy of the written page, their hard, emotional shells crack open to reveal the uncertainty that comes from not knowing if their father has any interest in them. The stories are like letters to unknown dads—some filled with imaginary scenes about what it might be like to have a dad who comes home and puts his arm around you or plays with you.

They feel like they've been thrown away, Mr. Myers says, because "they don't have a father to push them, discipline them, and they give up trying to succeed . . . they don't see themselves as wanted." A regular theme is that they feel safer in a foster-care home or juvenile detention center than on the outside, because they have no father to hold together the family.

The extent of the problem is clear. The nation's out-of-wedlock birth rate is 38 percent. Among white children, 28 percent are now born to a single mother; among Hispanic children it is 50 percent, and it reaches a chilling, disorienting peak of 71 percent for black children. According to the National Center for Health Statistics, nearly a quarter of America's white children (22 percent) do not have any male in their homes; nearly a third (31 percent) of Hispanic children and over half of black children (56 percent) are fatherless.

This represents a dramatic shift in American life. In the early 1960s, only 2.3 percent of white children and 24 percent of black children were born to a single mom. Having a dad, in short, is now a privilege, a ticket to middle-class status on par with getting into a good college.

Studies confirm that the daily presence of a father in a child's life leads to decreased negative behaviors like involvement in drugs and violence and an increase in positive behavior such as improved academic performance. *Courtesy of David Turnley/Corbis*

The odds increase for a child's success with the psychological and financial stability rooted in having two parents. Having two parents means there is a greater likelihood that someone will read to a child as a preschooler, support him through school, and prevent him from dropping out, as well as teaching him how to compete, win and lose, and get up to try again, in academics, athletics, and the arts. Maybe most important of all is that having a dad at home is almost a certain ticket out of poverty, because about 40 percent of single-mother families are in poverty.

"If you are concerned about reducing child poverty then you have to focus on missing percent of the "baby's daddy" spent time with the child or took "a lot" of interest in the baby. That is quite a contrast to the married black mothers who told researchers that 88 percent of married black men, or men living with the mother, regularly spent time with the child and took responsibility for the child's well-being.

In his fictional books, Walter Dean Myers has found that the key to reaching young readers is to connect with their "internal life of insecurities and doubts."

More so today than in the past, reaching the heart of insecurity among young people means writing about the hurt of life without a dad. It also means writing about being young and black

> Having a dad, in short, is now a privilege, a ticket to middle-class status on par with getting into a good college.

fathers," says Roland Warren, president of the National Fatherhood Initiative, based in Gaithersburg, Maryland.

The odds are higher that a child without a dad will have more contact with the drug culture, the police, and jail. Even in kindergarten, children living with single parents are more likely to trail children with two parents when it comes to health, cognitive skills, and their emotional maturity. They are in the back of the bus before the bus—their life—even gets going.

A study of black families ten years ago, when the out-of-wedlock birth rate was not as high as today, found that single moms reported only 20 or brown in the midst of the flood of negative images in rap videos without a positive male role model. These young people see so many others just like them standing on street corners, unconnected to family life and failing at school and work and threatening violence—and in so many cases, just like them, without an adult male to guide them.

In his own life, Mr. Myers often looked down on the man in his house: his stepfather, who worked as a janitor and was illiterate. He felt this man had little to teach him.

Then his own son complained one day that he, Myers, "sounded just like granddad" when he told the boy to pick up after himself, to work harder and show respect to people.

"I didn't know it at the time," says Mr. Myers of his stepfather, "but just having him around meant I was picking up his discipline, his pride, his work ethic." He adds: "Until I heard it from my son I never understood it."

Juan Williams, one of America's leading political commentators and writers, is the author of the critically acclaimed biography *Thurgood Marshall—American Revolutionary.* He is also the author of the nonfiction bestseller *Eyes on the Prize: America's Civil Rights Years, 1954–1965,* the companion volume to the critically acclaimed television series. His most recent book is *Enough: The Phony Leaders, Dead-End Movements, and Culture of Failure That Are Undermining Black America—and What We Can Do About It.*

Williams is also the senior correspondent for National Public Radio and political analyst for the Fox News Channel. He is a regular panelist on the weekly news affairs program *Fox News Sunday* and the host of the syndicated TV news show *America's Black Forum.* Articles by Williams have appeared in magazines ranging from *Newsweek, Fortune,* and *the Atlantic Monthly* to *Ebony, Gentlemen's Quarterly,* and the *New Republic.*

((ACTIONS SPEAK LOUDEST: FATHERHOOD

The National Center for Educational Statistics reported that when fathers are involved, their children are more likely to get A's, enjoy school, and participate in extracurricular activities. Conversely, when fathers are absent, the children have a higher rate of asthma, depression, and behavioral problems, while teenagers are at greater risk of alcohol use, drug use, and suicide. Below are some ways to help ensure that more children realize the benefits of having a father figure in their lives.

IN MY HOME
I CAN . . .

Carve out a special "father and child" time or activity every day.

It is easy to get caught up in life's many responsibilities, with quality "play" time falling to the bottom of the to-do list. If you are a father or a father figure, be sure to set aside time every day to do something special with the child in your life. Throw the ball around, read a book or the paper, talk about sports or music, or just take a walk.

Find positive male role models for my child.

If there is not a father or father figure in your home, try to connect your child with a positive male role model, from your own father to a friend to a respected member of your community. Maybe even sign your child up for a "big brother" at www.bbbs.org.

Celebrate great fathers.

It doesn't have to be Father's Day to show appreciation for your dad or the father figures in your life. Pick up the phone, send a card, thank your father for the ways that he has contributed to who you are as an adult. Or help your children do the same for the father figures in their lives.

IN OUR COMMUNITIES
WE SHOULD . . .

Participate in programs that bring fathers and children together.
The Take Our Daughters and Sons to Work Day program is a wonderful way to share time
with a child and help him or her envision a future. Encourage your workplace to participate
in the program and be sure to bring the child in your life to work.

Become male role models.
Volunteer to coach a sports team, lead a program at your local community center, or mentor a child. Visit www.volunteermatch.org to find opportunities in your local area.

IN OUR COUNTRY
YOU COULD . . .

Support organizations that support fatherhood.
The National Fatherhood Initiative's (NFI) mission is to improve the well-being of children
by increasing the proportion of children growing up with involved, responsible, and committed fathers. For more information or to contribute to or volunteer for their effort, visit www
.fatherhood.org.

**Encourage policymakers and leaders to make sure that America's fathers stay
involved in their children's lives.**
The federal government spent at least $99.8 billion providing assistance to father-absent
families in 2006. NFI's Task Forces on Responsible Fatherhood aims to provide our lawmakers with the knowledge and resources they need to make informed decisions about
legislation that will affect children and families. You can encourage your congressperson
to join the task force at www.fatherhood.org/taskforces.asp.

Despite limited income and means, this mother's house was a de facto home for both her own children and for many unsupervised children in her small town. *Courtesy of Ann Weathersby*

MOTHERHOOD))

Angeline Lee

ANGELINE LEE

Motherhood changed me. There is nothing else in this world that has been able to change the core of the person that I am like the experiences of being a mother.

I was raised by a single mom. Being only twenty-one at the time I was born, my mother did all she knew to care for me. She went back to school. She tried to work, but after a number of frightening experiences with various child care providers, my mother made the decision to remain home with me. As a result, we became dependent on welfare and subsidized housing assistance to help us live.

It was hard for us. I can remember times when food was scarce in our home, when sandwiches consisting of white bread and Miracle Whip were graciously consumed to nourish my body. I remember times of catching the city bus with my mom to get to appointments in the snow. One day, while running to get to the bus before it left the stop, I lost my boot in the deep Midwestern snow. This was our life.

Shortly after we had to sell our car to pay the bills, I had an evening program at my school. I was given the rather minuscule role of holding up a sign containing an image of the sun during one of the songs. Not having transportation usually meant that I was not able to participate in extracurricular or after-school events. However, my mother, realizing how important that night

was for me, humbled herself and borrowed her old car from the neighbor she sold it to and took me to the program at school. Even though I was no more than seven years old at the time, I literally can still feel the pride in my chest when my cue came to hold up the sun.

My mother loved me. And through her struggles raising me alone, she continuously relayed that love to me through her actions. Yes, it was hard for her. But in her challenging circumstance, she did all she knew to give me the best she could.

As I fast-forward through time I stop at the moment my first child was born. The discomforts and pains of pregnancy and labor held nothing over the love and adoration I felt for that little child. As I looked into his eyes and welcomed him into my world, I knew that I had to be the best I could for him because he had been given to me by God. And that same awe was present at the birth of my second child. A steady gaze into her eyes also birthed something in me. It was at those moments of connection that I dedicated myself to encourage each of them to be the best they could be in every aspect of their lives, like my mom did for me.

I do not want my children to become another common statistic of everything wrong in the world. My children will not join the masses in the daily consumption of junk. They will not willingly be placed in front of a television screen dictating to them that the ills of society should be welcomed and embraced. I closely monitor what foods they eat and drink. I consistently watch what media images they are exposed to. However, despite my well-intentioned quest to raise my children above the status quo, I constantly have to battle through challenges and obstacles.

The sheer cost of eating healthy at times has been prohibitive in maintaining the diet I want for them. The cost of a daily diet that includes a variety of fresh fruits and vegetables is both a challenge and an obstacle. I cannot always afford to eat the way I know is best for us. Accepting that as my reality is hard. The cost of provid-

hurting the emotional development of those beautiful babies whose eyes I looked into and made a promise for life. When I realized that my fears were functioning at a higher place in my life than the sacred promise I made to those babies, I prayed to God for strength and I allowed myself to be put on a course of healing and restoration. That course helped me to acknowledge my own contributions to the challenges and obstacles I've faced. For me, difficult times open up an environment where I can easily lose focus on self-building actions and activities and redirect my energy to self-destructive ones such as overeating and being sedentary. Of course, how I live my own life directly influences and impacts the lives of my children.

> I do not want my children to become another common statistic of everything wrong in the world.

ing my children with a basic necessity like food should not be a hindrance to feeding them what is best for their health. But for myself, and many others, it has been.

Like too many of us, my first marriage did not work out. As I processed through the situation there were many mental and emotional battles that attempted to rule over my life. However, it was the damage being done to my children that gave me the strength to fight for my life. I understood that it was my choices that were

Even through difficult times, it is a beautiful experience for me to know that the children who continually encourage me to live better for them have now adopted that same belief system for themselves. They realize that from what they eat to how they treat others to how they expect to be treated are all important. They know that wise choices and healthy living are normal and expected parts of their lives. And because those are part of who they are, they will carry that mentality with them into adulthood and parenthood.

And so, as we look forward to the life that our children, grandchildren, great-grandchildren, and more may lead, many may consider the question of where does the positive change in direction for our future generations truly begin. I believe with all of my heart that change in the lives of our future generations begins within each of us.

Angeline Lee of Pasadena, California, is the mother of two active children—a son and a daughter.

Lee is enthusiastic about her goals in life, but isn't shy about sharing previous hardships she has endured, such as hunger. She is proud to have overcome a childhood that at times involved eating as much as possible in one sitting because there was not enough food in her home growing up.

Lee is featured as a Champion for Change and a Hero Mom in the new *Network for a Healthy California* advertising campaign, which emphasizes the importance of fruit and vegetable consumption and physical activity.

(((ACTIONS SPEAK LOUDEST: MOTHERHOOD

More so than any other single person, the daily decisions made by mothers have the most profound impact on our children. And at the same time, they face significant challenges that we as a society have too often failed to address. From the millions of mothers trying to juggle the responsibilities of a career while raising a family, to the rising numbers of single mothers having to do it all alone, we need to find better ways to assist mothers in overcoming these challenges. Below are a few suggestions worth considering when looking at the role of mothers today.

IN MY HOME
I CAN . . .

Spend focused time with my family.
Studies show that spending just one hour a day talking to your children improves academic performance and decreases negative behavior. Having regular family dinners will help ensure that you're spending quality time with and talking to your children in a comfortable environment.

Make time for myself.
Reducing your stress will help reduce your children's stress. Getting thirty minutes of physical activity a day will help increase your energy, your mood, and your health. Try going for a quick walk before, during, or after your workday. To learn about what other moms are doing for themselves and their families, visit Champions for Change at www.cachampions forchange.net/en/ChampionMoms.php.

IN OUR COMMUNITIES
WE SHOULD . . .

Support each other.

There may be some truth to the notion that it takes a village to raise a child. A local support system is an effective way to share the ups and downs of life with other mothers (search for local groups at www.singlemom.com). You can start a mothers' collaborative in your community (a carpool network) or reach out to other moms online. Blogs—written by moms—share tips to keep your family organized, list coupons for shopping online, and provide ideas for career choices. Start blogging at www.blogamama.com or look into other helpful resources at www.cafemom.com.

Seek out community-based programs.

Get involved with programs such as CATCH Kids Club (Coordinated Approach To Child Health) (www.catchinfo.org/index.asp) or the School Food Challenge (www.lunchlessons .org/html_v2/food_challenge.html). They're great ways to make nutrition interesting and physical activity fun for your community.

IN OUR COUNTRY
YOU COULD . . .

Advocate for Paid Family Leave.

The balance between work and family is one that with an expanding work week and rising expenses becomes increasingly hard to maintain. People often face a choice between the two. Current federal legislation allows for leave without pay, but this is often not practical for working parents. Contact your local federal legislator to see if they support efforts to ensure that parents or soon-to-be parents get paid leave.

Encourage your employer to adopt policies that help mothers in the workplace.

There are organizations that focus on the integral role that women play in the workforce. You can connect an organization like the Center for Work-Life Policy (www.worklifepolicy .org) with your employer. They help companies utilize their best practices in reaching women in non traditional circumstances and making the workplace a flexible and friendly one for mothers.

A FINAL THOUGHT

How wonderful it is that nobody need wait a single moment before starting to improve the world.

—Anne Frank

These words were written by a then-ordinary thirteen-year-old girl living during extraordinarily difficult times. In the face of such daunting circumstances, her simple expression should serve as a clarion call during our current challenges.

Our individual and collective legacies are not something that we should wait to reflect back on twenty years from now, but something that we should start creating today. Within these pages are hundreds of suggested calls to action on what you could do today, at this moment, to follow the admonition of this courageous young girl. Pick one, any one, and start now. Let your actions speak loudest.

We have created a community online, www.actionsspeakloudest.org, to help. There you will be able to share your ideas and actions about what you're doing to create a better world for this and future generations. By joining others who are committed to keeping our generational promise, you can see how your actions are helping add up to create a larger social impact on the issues in this book and others that community members identify.

You have already started making a difference by buying this book, as all of the authors' proceeds are going back into the issues and organizations featured in these pages. Let this be the start of your involvement in *Actions Speak Loudest*, not the end. Vincent van Gogh once wrote, "Great things are done by a series of small things brought together." What will we bring together today?

ACKNOWLEDGMENTS

My first gratitude is to you the reader. It is only through your support and actions that we will be able to keep our generational promise of leaving to our children a better world than we have inherited from our parents.

I wish to extend my deepest thanks to each of our contributors, whose words, ideas, and actions continue to inspire us all. Their individual legacies have long been established, and my appreciation for their collective support and faith in this project is beyond words. To put it simply, it has been an honor to be in their company on this project. A special note of appreciation goes to Juan Williams for his general support of this project and specifically for contributing the moving and insightful foreword to this collection.

Beside each of these esteemed contributors, often beyond the public eye, is a group of equally impressive individuals who have helped make their participation in this project possible. I would like to thank the following individuals for their time, cooperation, and patience during this process: Rachel Botsman, Michelle Boxer, Michelle Brunner, Rich Burg, Rose Capasso, Ann Christiano, Deanna Congileo, Louise Kennedy Converse, Jennifer Coppola, Joseph DeSantis, Charlie Dougiello, Michelle Evermore, Kirk Fisher, Marie Florio, Deborah Foley, Robin Giampa, Maury Gostfrand, Robert Govan III, Michelle Greco, Mary Hagerty, Michael Harney, Mary Kay Hort, Sharon Hunley, Sherry John, Frankie Jones, Alexander Kafka, Kathryn Kahler Vose, Andrew Kaplan, Jenelle Krishnamoorthy, Rebecca Larson, Kyu-Young Lee, Autumn Lennon, Dan Levy, Marty Lipp, Barbara Lopez, Elizabeth Majestic, Kate Medina, Patti Miller, Michelle Mussuto, Courtney O'Donnell, Lindsay Olsen, Cindy Paladines, David Park, Jay Paterno, Susan Pennel, Lee Perselay, Mike Poorman, Michelle Quint, Karen Redlener, Sandy Rinck, Karina Ron, Katy Rose, Tod Seisser, Pam Smith, Jan Spielberger, Tina Spurber, Ina Stern, Andrew M. Stroth, Kevin Sullivan, Heather Tamarkin, Megan Torres, Tim Ware, Jim Whitmire, Delise Williams, Kathy Williams, Virginia Witt, Ben Yarrow, Barbara Zadina, and Lydia Zelaya.

Our contributors extend beyond those who have contributed their ideas to those who have contributed their remarkable images to help bring these issues to life. I would like to thank all of them for capturing in photography what words sometimes cannot. A special thanks goes to David Turnley, whose early support for this project and willingness to donate his incredible work set the tone for all of our image selections. My gratitude also goes to my friend, Mike Burns, for making the introduction to David. I wish to extend my thanks to the wonderful team at Corbis for their tremendous flexibility and generosity in securing the majority of our images. Starting with Shawn Carkonen and extending to Arthur Felder and Kyle Whitehead, they have been an absolute pleasure to work with and I am grateful for their assistance. Several of our images have been donated by other photographers whom I would also like to thank for their generosity: Geoffrey George, Yuki Tripp Ogawa, Tyrone Turner, Ann Weathersby, and Amy Zachmeyer.

Pulling together a project of this size and scope took an incredibly dedicated group of individuals. I owe an immense debt to our team at YELLOWBRICKROAD who gave such invaluable assistance in coordinating the hundreds of moving parts of this manuscript, researching and drafting our "Actions Speak Loudest" content, and working with and coordinating the involvement of our contributors. To Jennifer Gilhooley, Jennifer Liguori, Shapel Mallard, Paris Martin, Danayi Munyati, Meagan Palatino, Meredith Ryan, Wendy Stewart, and Liza Vadnai my warmest thanks. Beyond their contributions, their support and indefatigable attitude throughout this process have been truly impressive. A special word of appreciation to Wendy, whose patience throughout this process has been matched only by her passion and spirit of partnership, by which she has helped bring this all together. I would also like to thank Ed Stein for lending us his watchful and diligent eye in reviewing this manuscript and Shay Fu for her early creative contributions on the cover design. My appreciation also goes out to our friends at Sol Design for their work on actionsspeakloudest.org.

This work would not be possible without my agent, Sorche Fairbank, who was a true champion for this project from the beginning to the end and who found it the perfect home at Globe Pequot Press. My many thanks to my editor, Mary Norris, whose input and support have been of tremendous value. Collectively, through their support and ideas, Sorche and Mary have elevated the potential impact of *Actions Speak Loudest*, without once undermining its integrity. Thanks also to Ann Courcy, Melissa Evarts, Sheryl Kober, Bob Sembiante, and Jennifer Taber at Globe Pequot Press.

On a more personal note, I would like to thank my grandmother Jessie Proctor, mother Daytona Roth, brother George Blair, and sister Lisa Leiphart for their continued inspiration. Too many of the issues covered in this book were ones that we as a family have had to face. Helen Keller once wrote, "Although the world is full of suffering, it is full also of the overcoming of it." They are "the overcoming." My appreciation for the quiet dignity and rugged determination with which they have had to overcome life's challenges is without limit. Thank you. Thank you. Thank you.

A debt of gratitude also goes out to all my friends and family, whose continued support for the work that we do at YELLOWBRICKROAD in general, and specifically this project, has been so uplifting. My thanks specifically to my best friend of almost thirty years, Laurence Mullaney, whose diligent encouragement has been a constant buoy, reminding me to pursue my passions and to find happiness in making a difference in this world.

Finally, my deepest gratitude is reserved for my wife, Julie McKinnon. As I write this in our daughter's nursery, I cannot help but be amazed by the level of love and support she has shown over the five years it has taken this project to transcend from the idea within my head to the printed page you now read. Never once did she waiver in her belief that this idea would become a reality. She has sacrificed much and received too little credit. I am truly blessed to have such an incredible partner in life. Everything good in my life, I owe in part to her. This is as much her book as it is mine. To Julie and our little champ Carlin, "more today."

CREDITS

Some of our contributors chose to use excerpts from previous writing and speeches as source materials from which their essays were adapted.

Carter, Jimmy. *The Nobel Peace Prize Lecture*. New York: Simon & Schuster, 2003.

Coles, Robert. *The Moral Intelligence of Children*. New York: Random House, 1997.

Eggers, Dave, Nínive Calegari, and Daniel Moulthrop. "Reading, Writing, Retailing," *New York Times*, June 27, 2005, p. 27.

Greene, Brian. "Put a Little Science in Your Life," *New York Times,* June 1, 2008, p. WK 14.

Kahlenberg, Richard D. "Cost Remains a Key Obstacle to College Access," *The Chronicle of Higher Education,* March 10, 2006, p. B51.

McKibben, Bill. "First, Step Up," *Yes!*, Spring 2008, p. 18–22.

———. "Introduction," in *Walden*. Boston: Beacon Press, 2004, p. vii–xxii.

The Saguaro Seminar. *Better Together, The Report of the Saguaro Seminar: Civic Engagement in America.* Cambridge, MA: John F. Kennedy School of Government, Harvard University, 2000.

Williams, Juan. "The Tragedy of America's Disappearing Fathers," *The Wall Street Journal,* June 14, 2008, p. A11.

Photo Credits

Photograph of Richard Castaldo, courtesy of David Salyer.

Photograph of Robert Coles, courtesy of Micah Marty.

Photograph of Dave Eggers, Nínive Calegari, and Daniel Moulthrop, courtesy of Meiko Takechi Arquillos.

Photograph of Joe Paterno, courtesy of Penn State Athletics Communications.

Photograph of Joe Torre, courtesy of Josh Sailor Photography.

Biography Credit

Biography for Newt Gingrich, courtesy of Callista Gingrich, Gingrich Productions.

RESOURCES

OUR CONTRIBUTOR ORGANIZATIONS

826 National: www.826national.org

Afterschool and Community Learning Network: www.afterschoolcommunitylearning.org

American Solutions for Winning the Future: www.americansolutions.com

Blue Shield of California Foundation: www.blueshieldcafoundation.org

The Boys' Club of New York: www.bcny.org

Campaign for a Commercial-Free Childhood: www.commercialfreechildhood.org

The Carter Center: www.cartercenter.org

The Century Foundation: www.tcf.org

Children & Nature Network: www.childrenandnature.org

Children's Health Fund: www.childrenshealthfund.org

Donovan McNabb Foundation: www.donovanmcnabb.com

The Early Childhood and Family Learning Foundation: www.lphi.org

The Earth Institute at Columbia University: www.earth.columbia.edu

Earth's Elders: www.earthselders.org

EmpowerME: www.empowerme2b.org

Harlem Children's Zone: www.hcz.org

Harvard University: www.harvard.edu

Joe Torre Safe at Home Foundation: www.joetorre.org

Judge Baker Children's Center: www.jbcc.harvard.edu

King Hussein Foundation: www.kinghusseinfoundation.org

KnowledgeWorks Foundation: www.kwfdn.org

Mia Hamm Foundation: www.miafoundation.org

National Public Radio: www.npr.org

The Network for a Healthy California (Champions for Change): www.cachampionsforchange.net

Noor Al Hussein Foundation: www.nooralhusseinfoundation.org

Operation HOPE, Inc.: www.operationhope.org

Penn State University: www.psu.edu

Robert Wood Johnson Foundation: www.rwjf.org

The Saguaro Seminar: www.hks.harvard.edu/saguaro

Step It Up 2007: http://stepitup07.org

Timberland: www.timberland.com

Yum-O! Foundation: www.yum-o.org

OTHER ORGANIZATIONS FOR YOUR REFERENCE

4Girls GLocal Leadership: www.4ggl.org

21st Century Community Learning Centers: www.21stcenturyskills.org

Above the Influence: www.abovetheinfluence.com

Advocates For Youth: www.advocatesforyouth.org

Albert Einstein Institution: www.aeinstein.org

All For Good: www.allforgood.org

The Alliance for a Healthier Generation: www.healthiergeneration.org

Alliance of Civilizations Media Fund: www.aocmediafund.org

American Academy of Pediatrics: www.aap.org

American Association of Retired Persons: www.aarp.org

American Community Gardening Association: www.communitygarden.org

American Red Cross: www.redcross.org

American Solutions for Winning the Future: www.americansolutions.com

American Youth Soccer Organization: www.soccer.org

Americans with Disabilities Act: www.ada.gov

America's Promise Alliance: www.americaspromise.org

AmeriCorps: www.americorps.gov

Arab West Foundation: www.arabwestfoundation.com

Arlington National Cemetery: www.arlingtoncemetery.org

The Bacchus Network: www.bacchusgamma.org

Big Brothers Big Sisters: www.bbbs.org

Bill & Melinda Gates Foundation: www.gatesfoundation.org

BlogaMama: www.blogamama.com

Boss of Me Inc.: www.bom411.com

Boy Scouts of America National Council: www.scouting.org

Boys & Girls Clubs of America: www.bgca.org

Break the Cycle: www.breakthecycle.org

Bridges to Understanding: www.bridgesweb.org

Business Ethics magazine: www.business-ethics.com

CafeMom: www.cafemom.com

Campaign for a Commercial-Free Childhood: www.commercialexploitation.org

Carbonrally: www.carbonrally.com

The Carnegie Foundation for the Advancement of Teaching: www.carnegiefoundation.org

Center for Media Literacy: www.medialit.org

Center for Work-Life Policy: www.worklifepolicy.org

Centers for Disease Control and Prevention: www.cdc.gov

Change.org: www.change.org

Childhelp: www.childhelp.org

Children Now: www.childrennow.org

Children of the Earth United: www.childrenoftheearth.org

Children's Disability Information: www.childrensdisabilities.info

Cinéma Vérité: www.cinema-verite.org

Citizens Against Government Waste: www.cagw.org

City Year: www.cityyear.org

Common Sense Media: www.commonsensemedia.org

Community Food Security Coalition: www.foodsecurity.org

The Concord Coalition: www.concordcoalition.org

Cooperative Grocers' Information Network: www.cgin.coop

Coordinated Approach to Child Health: www.catchinfo.org

Coordinated School Health Programs: www.cdc.gov/healthyYouth/CSHP/

Corporate Responsibility Officer: www.thecro.com

Creative Kids at Home: www.creativekidsathome.com

The Date Safe Project: www.thedatesafeproject.org

Do Something: www.dosomething.org

The Early College High School Initiative: www.earlycolleges.org

Earth 911: http://earth911.com

Edutopia: www.edutopia.org

EVERYBODY WINS!: www.everybodywins.org

Experience Corps: www.experiencecorps.org

Families USA: www.familiesusa.org

The Family Violence Prevention Fund: www.endabuse.org

Family Voices: www.familyvoices.org

Federal Communications Commission: www.fcc.gov

Federal Trade Commission Bureau of Consumer Protection: www.ftc.gov/bcp/consumer.shtm

Feeding America: http://feedingamerica.org

The Foundation for a Better Life: www.values.com

Fox Networks Group: www.fox.com/pause

Free the Children: www.freethechildren.com

GEAR UP: www.ed.gov/programs/gearup

Generations United: www.gu.org

Gettysburg.com: www.gettysburg.com

Girl Scouts of America: www.girlscouts.org

Global Issues: http://globalissues.org

Global Peace Film Festival: www.peacefilmfest.org

Googol Learning: www.googolpower.com

The Green Index: www.thegreenindex.com

Habitat for Humanity: www.habitat.org

HandsOn Network: www.handsonnetwork.org

HealthierUS.gov: www.healthierus.gov

The High Purpose Company, by Christine Arena: www.high-purpose.com

House Committee on Education & Labor: http://edlabor.house.gov

IBM: www.ibm.com

Idealist: www.idealist.org

International Day of Peace: www.international dayofpeace.org

International Play Association: www.ipaworld.org

International Walk to School: www.iwalkto school.org

The Internet Public Library: www.ipl.org

Josephson Institute for Sports Ethics: http://josephsoninstitute.org/sports

The Journal of the American Medical Association: http://jama.ama-assn.org

JumpStart Coalition for Financial Literacy: www.jumpstartcoalition.org

Junior Achievement: www.ja.org

KaBOOM!: www.kaboom.org

Kaiser Family Foundation: www.kff.org

KidSites.com: www.kidsites.com

KidzWorld: www.kidzworld.com

King Hussein Foundation: www.kinghussein foundation.org

KIPP: www.kipp.org

Liz Claiborne: www.lizclaiborne.com

McGill University's Middle East Program in Civil Society and Peace Building: www.mcgill.ca/mmep

Men's Network Against Domestic Violence: www.menagainstdv.org

Mentor: www.mentoring.org

Mickelson ExxonMobil Teachers Academy: www.exxonmobil.com/corporate/community_ed_math_academy.aspx

Millennium Promise: www.millenniumpromise.org

Model School Wellness Policies: www.school wellnesspolicies.org

The Muscular Dystrophy Association: www.mda.org

Music for Youth Foundation: www.musicfor youth.org

National Alliance for Nutrition & Activity: www.cspinet.org/nutritionpolicy/nana.html

National Alliance for Youth Sports: www.nays.org

National Association of Student Councils: www.nasc.us

National Center for Education Statistics: http://nces.ed.gov/

The National Center for Victims of Crime: www.ncvc.org

The National Center on Addiction and Substance Abuse at Columbia University: www.casacolumbia.org

National Commission on Teaching and America's Future: www.nctaf.org

National Conference of State Legislatures: www.ncsl.org

National Disability Sports Alliance: www.blazesports.org

National Education Association: www.nea.org

National Fatherhood Initiative: www.fatherhood.org

National Geographic: www.nationalgeographic.com

National Heart, Lung, and Blood Institute: www.nhlbi.nih.gov

National Math and Science Initiative: www.nationalmathandscience.org

National Park Service: www.nps.gov

National Priorities Project: www.nationalpriorities.org

National Wildlife Federation: www.nwf.org

National Youth Science Foundation: www.nysf.com

National Youth Violence Prevention Resource Center: www.safeyouth.org

Network for Good: www.networkforgood.org

NFL Rush: www.nflrush.com

NYC Teaching Fellows: www.nycteachingfellows.org

Official City Sites.org: http://officialcitysites.org

ONE Campaign: www.one.org

Parent Teacher Association: www.pta.org

Pathways to Peace: www.pathwaystopeace.org

PBS Kids: www.pbskids.org

Peaceful Schools International: www.peacefulschoolsinternational.org

Quest Magazine: www.questmag.com

Regulations.gov: www.regulations.gov

Rescuing Recess: www.rescuingrecess.com

Sallie Mae: www.salliemae.com

The School Food Challenge: www.lunchlessons.org

Share Our Strength: www.strength.org

Sierra Club: www.sierraclub.org

SingleMom.com: www.singlemom.com

Smithsonian Education: www.smithsonianeducation.org

Southern Poverty Law Center: www.splcenter.org

Special Needs Alliance: www.specialneedsalliance.com

Special Olympics: www.specialolympics.org

Spot the Block: www.spottheblock.com

State Children's Health Insurance Program: www.cms.hhs.gov

Stop Bullying Now!: http://stopbullyingnow.hrsa.gov

Student Pledge Against Gun Violence: www.pledge.org

Substance Abuse & Mental Health Services Administration: www.samhsa.gov

Take Our Daughters and Sons to Work
Foundation: www.daughtersandsons
towork.org

Take Your Kids 2 Vote: www.takeyourkids2vote
.org

Talk with Your Kids: www.talkingwithkids.org

Teach for America: www.teachforamerica.org

Teach Kids How: www.teachkidshow.com

Three Cups of Tea: www.threecupsoftea.com

TIME for Kids: www.timeforkids.com/tfk/kids

TreeHugger: www.treehugger.com

TRIO: www.ed.gov/about/offices/list/ope/trio/
index.html

Truth: www.thetruth.com

Turn Off Your TV: www.turnoffyourtv.com

United Nations: www.un.org

United World Colleges: www.uwc.org

U.S. Department of Education: www.ed.gov

U.S. Department of Health & Human Services:
www.hhs.gov

U.S. Food and Drug Administration: www.fda
.gov

U.S. Government Bookstore:
http://bookstore.gpo.gov

U.S. House of Representatives: www.house.gov

U.S. Senate Committee on Health, Education,
Labor, & Pensions: http://help.senate.gov

The UTeach Institute: www.uteach-institute.org

VERB: www.cdc.gov/youthcampaign

Volunteer Match: www.volunteermatch.org

The World Peace Prayer Society:
www.worldpeace.org

YMCA: www.ymca.net

Youth Noise: www.youthnoise.com

INDEX

W. Callaghan

Bill

Jimmy Carter

Newt Gingrich

Crystal H. Eg

Robert D. Kalkenberg

James R. Works

Terry K. Peterson

Joe Paterno

Pat Cooper

Jeffrey S. Swartz